THE VIRGIN
UNIVERSITY
SURVIVAL GUIDE

Also published by Virgin Books:

The Virgin Alternative Guide to British Universities
The Student Cookbook
The Student Vegetarian Cookbook
The Virgin Traveller's Handbook

THE VIRGIN UNIVERSITY SURVIVAL GUIDE

KARLA FITZHUGH

This edition first published in Great Britain in 2007 by
Virgin Books Ltd
Thames Wharf Studios
Rainville Road
London
W6 9HA

First published in Great Britain in 2004 by Virgin Books Ltd

A catalogue record for this book is available from the British Library.

ISBN 978 0 7535 1248 7

The Random House Group Limited supports The Forest Stewardship Council (FSC), the leading international forest certification organisation. All our titles that are printed on Greenpeace approved FSC certified paper carry the FSC logo. Our paper procurement policy can be found at: www.rbooks.co.uk/environment

Mixed Sources
Product group from well-managed
forests and other controlled sources
www.fsc.org Cert no. TT-COC-2139
© 1996 Forest Stewardship Council
FSC

Typeset by Phoenix Photosetting, Chatham, Kent
Printed in the UK by CPI Bookmarque, Croydon, CR0 4TD

CONTENTS

INTRODUCTION

You made it! You're starting a university course, probably at the end of the summer. Fame, fortune and debauchery await. OK, so I lied about the money bit. It's going to be a roller-coaster ride of good times and hard work, and hopefully you'll come out of it at the end with a top-class degree and bright career prospects.

It's an enormous financial commitment, so you might just want to get a decent degree out of it. You're totally responsible for your own workload, in spite of all those wonderful distractions that are constantly going on around you. Putting some effort in right from the beginning pays dividends later and it's useful to know how to stay motivated, or where to go for extra help and information at times when you get a bit stuck.

Going to university is about much more than academic qualifications. Strong friendships are forged and your social life and love life will probably take off like a rocket. Student life can sometimes be stressful, so along with your living situation, your overdraft and that overdue essay, it's good to know that there's a big support network of university advisors, careers counsellors, health staff and representatives from the National Union of Students to back you up.

It's all there waiting for you. Enjoy!

CHAPTER 1: GETTING READY

Starting at university tends to be the first time that students have lived away from home for any long period, and there can be a steep learning curve. Prepare for what lies ahead:

- **Strike a balance when packing**
- **Keep paperwork together in a safe place**
- **Pick up life skills: cooking, laundry, finances**
- **Pay some thought to people you're leaving behind**
- **Arrangements: insurance, accommodation, student bank account**

STUDYING NEAR TO HOME

There is an increasing trend for students to apply for degree courses in their home town. If you do stay with your family at university, it's cheaper and more comfortable. On the other hand, it may feel harder to meet new people or your parents' rules may annoy you. You still need to open a student account and maybe put together a small cash fund.

SOMEWHERE TO LAY YOUR HEAD

Once you've been accepted onto your course, start arranging accommodation. If possible, talk to someone who attended the university recently and knows the halls etc. Chat to current students on message boards of websites. Just remember, wherever you pick won't be the Ritz.

If your priorities are convenience and making lots of friends, then go for a big hall on campus, perhaps with its own bar or social rooms. If you want somewhere quieter, try for a place in a university-owned house slightly away from the main campus.

Sometimes a university has more students arriving each year than they can actually house and a few unlucky students unexpectedly find themselves in temporary accommodation, living miles out of town with an unfamiliar family, or even sleeping on camp beds on the floor of the gym. If it happens to you, do your best to grin and bear it; things will get sorted out eventually.

You may prefer to rent privately. Unless you're prepared to lodge or take a bedsit, you'll probably end up in a shared house because it's cheapest. Ask the accommodation office for a list of recommended housing agencies or landlords, and travel to the area and view properties, preferably with a friend or relative for safety. Or book a temporary room and then house hunt during your first few days in town. Meet the other tenants before you sign anything, as you could end up sharing with anyone.

Check what's provided by the university or your private landlord before you travel, so you don't end up buying or carrying anything you don't need.

- **Ask about bedlinen, duvets, towels, pans, kettles, crockery, cutlery, furniture, laundry facilities and telephone points.**

- **Ask about kitchen and bathroom facilities, canteen hours, cleaners and how many people you're sharing with.**

- **If you're bringing a car or a bike ask about parking places, bike stands, parking permits and security measures.**

- **Find out what bills you pay on top of your rent or hall fees, and how often.**

Once you have written proof of accommodation, get your belongings insured. For more details of insurance see the chapter on Freshers' week.

GET YOUR CASH INTO SHAPE
There are going to be several extra drains on your cash flow when you arrive, such as the enjoyments of freshers' week, buying basic household goods and groceries, and course books. Figure in the following:

Deposits for accommodation

Important reading list books

Stationery

Transport: bus passes, taxis, bikes, road tax, petrol

Groceries, kitchen equipment

Drinks, entry to clubs, cinemas, gigs

Fees for clubs and societies

Connection fees, payphones, mobile phone bill

Eating out

University fees

Whatever you think you'll spend on drinking, going out and other socialising, double it for a more realistic estimate.

Apply early for your maximum amount of student loan to help meet your living costs while you are studying. Contact your local award authority (not the place you will be studying at), for an application form for their means testing and eligibility assessments. Part, but not all, of this loan is means tested. For Student Loans Company details, see the Contacts section of this book.

Open a student bank account now, and save yourself hassle in freshers' week (see Chapter 6).

READY TO FEND FOR YOURSELF?
If you don't know much about handling finances, now's a good time to start. Learn how to make and stick to a basic budget (see the Money chapter later), and know how to write cheques or use bank or credit cards without getting ripped off. Get into the habit of putting enough to one side for bills. If you don't know how to check and pay bills, ask a relative or your local Citizens Advice Bureau (see Contacts section).

Computer skills are helpful, lasting through university and beyond. A fast typing speed can also grab you some of the better-paid part-time jobs.

If you aren't already used to doing your own laundry, it's another useful skill to have before you leave home. Parents will help you out, but if in doubt read the instructions inside the clothes, on the front of the washing machine or the laundry detergent packet (see Appendix for more).

You don't have to be the next celebrity chef, just get together a handful of simple recipes that don't need too many pans or gadgets. To get started in the kitchen, buy simple cookbooks such as *The Complete Cookery Course* by Delia Smith, BBC Consumer Publishing, £9.99 or *The Essential Student Cookbook* by Cas Clarke, Hodder Headline, £5.99.

You might prefer to live in a hovel that looks like a council tip, but try to keep it just above the dysentery line. Check the Appendix for idiot-proof cleaning tips.

FRIENDS, FAMILY AND GIRLFRIENDS/BOYFRIENDS

Moving to a new town means seeing less of your family, local friends or boyfriends or girlfriends back home. Lots of new students find this unsettling, but you can still keep in touch with old friends while you're making new ones. Check in every few days, and plan events to look forward to during holidays or mid-term weekends.

Boyfriends and girlfriends can become insecure if they're not going to the same college as you, and you may have to sit them down and talk it out. Long-distance relationships need both partners to make an equal amount of effort. If one of you isn't that committed, be honest and call it quits. Or you could both just see how it goes, acknowledging the fact that the university experience might change one or both of you, and that you might meet new people.

Mums and dads sometimes get a bit mopey or start to nag, especially if you have a very close family or you're the first or last offspring to leave home. Even if they're being totally embarrassing, try not to laugh at them or have an argument. Parents are bound to worry, even if they are proud of you getting a university place or it's high time you moved out anyway.

THINKING AHEAD

Do you need to make any arrangements with the university or other organisations before you arrive on their doorstep?

- **International students have extra activities laid on for them during freshers' week. Contact the university's International Office to find out about welcome schemes, assistance with immigration and funding issues.**

- **Mature students (anyone over the age of 21) are probably more than capable of looking after themselves, but may wish to live separately, or might be slightly rusty regarding studying. Try NIACE (www.niace.org.uk) or UCAS (www.ucas.com) for general advice.**

- **Students with children should contact the university childcare support officer about financial support and the university crèche, and organise back-up support with relatives and childminders in case of emergencies. Government support for UK undergraduate students with children includes the Childcare Grant and Dependants' Grant. Parents who are eligible should apply to their Local Education Authority (LEA) when they apply for general financial support (see www.dfes.gov.uk).**

- **Students with disabilities should call up to discuss any requirements ahead of time, and can benefit from contacting SKILL, the National Bureau for Students with Disabilities (see Contacts section). They provide advice on all aspects of student life, including welfare, work experience and volunteering, and they produce a range of guides.**

WHAT TO PACK (ESSENTIALS AND OTHER ITEMS)

The further you have to travel to university, the less you should weigh yourself down with. Stick to the bare essentials, then buy other items as you need them after you arrive. Pack a small bag with all essential paperwork.

BARE ESSENTIALS
ID: driving licence, passport, birth certificate

Train, bus or plane tickets

Discount railcard or coach card

Course acceptance letter

Course reading list etc.

Accommodation office letter

Insurance documents

Campus map

Several passport-size photos of yourself

Waterproof bag or folder for documents

Wallet, money, cash card

Bank details

Diary, or electronic organiser

Notepad and pen

Alarm clock

A few clothes

Rainproof jacket, umbrella

Addresses and contact numbers for next of kin, doctor and dentist back
   home

Glasses, contact lenses

Essential medication, contraception

Washbag, toiletries

Small first aid kit

Toilet roll, tissues

Small bag or rucksack

Bedlinen, bath towel (if needed)

USEFUL
Stereo and radio, CDs or MP3 player

Laptop or personal computer

Mobile phone

Hairdryer

Snacks for when you arrive

Mugs, tea, coffee and dried milk

Bowl, plate, cutlery

Enough clothes to last ten days

Sports kit

Dressing gown or towelling robe (for fire drills in the middle of the night)

Multi-function penknife

Bottle opener, can opener

Small torch

Pictures, posters, photos

OTHER ITEMS
Lamp

Bedspread, throws, cushions or rug

TV, video, DVD player, games console

Cheap or disposable camera

Clothes airer

Sandwich box

Kitchen equipment: pan with lid, frying pan, wooden spoon or spatula, small chopping board and knife, metal sieve, tea towel, washing up cloth

Calculator

Small stationery set

Clothes mending kit

Mini tool kit with flat head and Phillips screwdrivers

Books, folders, notepaper

Travel iron

After all this preparation, you're as ready as you'll ever be for freshers' week. Fasten those seatbelts.

CHAPTER 2: FRESHERS' WEEK

Ah, freshers' week. One thing's for sure – you won't be feeling fresh by the end of it. Be ready for:

- **Arriving at your accommodation and settling yourself in**
- **Doing a few chores**
- **An insane social calendar**
- **Making friends, meeting flatmates and course mates**

Expect long queues for everything, repetitive strain injury of your voice box from answering the same questions over and over again, industrial strength hangovers and the occasional tiny pang of homesickness.

TOUCHING DOWN ON PLANET UNI

If driving, arrive early to get a better parking place. If you've come in on the train or coach you'll probably have a few bags, so treat yourself to a taxi. Keep your maps and documents close to hand.

If you're staying in halls or university houses, you usually have to go to the accommodation office as your first port of call (sometimes you go straight to the hall). Show them your ID, and pick up your room or house number and keys. Everyone turns up at the same time, and you will have to queue.

Smile, say hello to all kinds of different students and make some small talk to pass the time. By the time you finally get keys and directions, you might have found out about a party that night or met someone off your course.

HI HONEY, I'M HOME

When you get to your hall or flat, you might need to sort out security codes for push-button locks on the front door, or a swipe card. Some halls also have telephone lines in each room where you have to sign up for a contract with the communications company on arrival. You'll also have an invitation (it's an order really) to attend an induction meeting, where they run you through essential information about security and fire escapes and so on, and you get to check out the cuties that have arrived that day. Learn the evacuation procedure for the fire alerts, including your escape route and meeting point, and rest assured there will be at least one practice drill soon. It is always in the middle of the night, so have clothes nearby to throw on quickly, and bring guests downstairs with you.

FIRST THINGS FIRST

When you get to your room, it will be bare and tiny. Get in there quickly and make it your own.

- **Make your bed up so you can go out then return to a ready bed.**
- **Brighten the place up and get those walls covered with at least one or two pics.**
- **If that doesn't quite do the trick, buy some cheap throws, rugs etc. later.**

Leave the door open while you unpack a few essential belongings so that you can see the other people who are moving in, but don't leave the room unattended. Get off on the right foot with students in your flat or corridor by smiling and saying hello, and introducing yourself. Dig out your coffee mugs and offer to make people a hot drink.

At this point pretty much everybody decides to go out to whatever entertainments have been laid on. More about partying later, let's get the housekeeping out of the way first.

NUS MEMBERSHIP

It isn't compulsory to join the National Union of Students, but it does offer a wide range of benefits from advice on all aspects of student life to cheap beer and discounts on books and records. You get an ID card with your NUS student number on it.

YOUR COURSE

There may be a set time in the week to formally enrol on your chosen degree course. The people in this queue are the people you're going to be crammed into lecture halls and tutorial rooms with for at least the next three years, so you might as well get to know them now. Pick up any timetables or other course information, such as a syllabus, and if there's something you don't understand, ask. There might be a departmental introduction or party too.

STUDENT HEALTH

Sign up with a nearby general practitioner or student health services. Think about signing up with a dentist if they're attached to student health or the nearby dental school, or arrange check-ups for when you go home during the holidays.

GIMME THE MONEY

Go to the finance office and sort out any student loans or bursaries as a priority. These cheques and money transfers could arrive late, so be prepared. Most banks will be sympathetic.

WHY BOTHER WITH INSURANCE?

If you haven't already arranged some insurance for your personal belongings, do so right now – students are targets for theft. Your parents' home contents insurance policy may cover you at university, but check the small print carefully. Items such as bicycles or laptop computers may attract a premium.

JOINING THE BOOK CLUB

If there's a guided tour of the main library go on it, and save hours of hassle in the long run. Find out where the main texts for your course are kept, along with reference books, theses, journals and magazines. Learn the procedures for ordering books and papers in from other libraries, and how to get items out of storage. While you're there, get a library card.

THE FRESHERS' WEEK ENTERTAINMENTS

Now for the fun bit. Freshers' week is about enjoying yourself and your new surroundings, and socialising like mad. The student union bar will be busy all week. Expect anything from cheesy club nights to organised pub crawls.

There will be gallons of cheap beer and perhaps some free promotional alcohol on top of that. You might also be offered drugs. Pace yourself, know the law and don't overdo things early in the evening or at the start of the week.

From a safety point of view, know where you're going that evening and how you're getting back. Don't walk home drunk in the dark on your own. Potential muggers and rapists can and do take advantage of the fact that students may be drunk during freshers' week. The university may run a safety bus to take female students back to their accommodation.

YOUR NEW BEST FRIENDS

If you were the shy one at school, so what? You have a clean slate and nobody knows you, so be whoever you want to be. Smile and say hello to people and strike up a few conversations, and you'll soon find that most people are slightly grateful when someone is friendly and takes an interest.

The conversations can be a bit repetitive at first. You may get sick of being asked where you're from, what course you're doing, where you're staying or what A levels you took. Break out of this by asking open questions: their taste in music or films, where they've travelled or what sports they're into. If you hit it off, swap names and emails or mobile phone numbers and keep in touch.

The people you spend time with in the first couple of days may not turn out to be the people you are firm friends with by the end of the term, but you never know. You can never have too many mates after all.

It's also a time when students meet new boyfriends or girlfriends. There's plenty of flirting, a fair amount of drunken snogging and a few one-night stands. Watch out for second and third years, who may be circling the bar looking for fresh faces.

CLUBS AND SOCIETIES

Get yourself along to the Societies Fair. The sillier-sounding societies are simply a great excuse for a party. The sports clubs tend to be focused towards team games such as football, hockey and rugby. There may also be a chance to try something like hang-gliding, potholing, scuba-diving, parachuting, flying or windsurfing – for a very small fee.

The societies can cover anything from the Lesbian, Gay and Bisexual Society (LGBSoc) to the Young Conservatives group, via the Home Brew Society and the Biology Society. If there's one for your subject area, make a point of signing up. They can offer anything from moral support to work experience. Join at least one or two clubs and societies, and pay your subscription fee.

HOMESICKNESS AND STRESS

Everything is new: people, surroundings, living conditions, rules and expectations. It's perfectly normal to feel overwhelmed by it at times. Everyone is feeling the same way to some extent, it's just that some of them are better at covering it up than others. It gets better with time.

Self-help for homesickness:

- **Call up mates or family back home for a chat.**

- **Break down difficult tasks into smaller, more manageable chunks.**

- **Eat regular meals and limit caffeine to prevent mood swings.**

- **Exercise is a proven mood booster.**

- **Avoid heavy drinking or street drugs.**

If things are getting too much for you, talk to someone. If you're feeling so anxious or depressed that you are having trouble eating or sleeping, get down to campus health or the university counselling service. They have years of experience helping students with these problems, plus it's all kept completely confidential.

CHAPTER 3: YOUR COURSE

At university, you're responsible for your attendance, workload, learning and overall performance. While this can take some getting used to, there is also the freedom of being your own boss.

This chapter will give you the lowdown on:

- **How to hit the ground running during your first term**

- **Some of the useful skills that you need to pick up**

- **The structure of university courses and dates**

- **Getting the best out of lectures, seminars and practicals**

- **Researching and writing top class assignments**

- **Passing those end-of-term exams with flying colours**

THE BASICS

GETTING STARTED
Some of the most important things:

- **Course content**
  Your department should provide you with a course guide, hopefully a comprehensive one that gives you a very specific idea of what topics will be covered, the skills you're expected to pick up and how your work will be assessed. Have a good look through it before you file it. Keep in a safe place because you'll need to check it, especially before exams.

- **Timetable**
  Make sure you have the most up-to-date version of your study timetable, with all the times and places of lectures, seminars and practicals listed.

Attend everything on your schedule, at least at the beginning of term, so you can find out what's truly compulsory. Keep a copy with you.

- **Your study area**
Make the area around your desk as work-friendly as possible. Pin up a list of your term's assignments and deadlines so you know what work is outstanding and how long you have to finish it. Your course content guide and administrative paperwork should be filed nearby for easy reference, along with lecture notes and other research.

- **Books**
You will have been given a huge book list, divided into main texts and other texts. You don't have to buy everything on the list. Discuss with a tutor or students in the years above you – don't rush out and buy the whole list. If it's an essential textbook then definitely buy one and make sure it's the latest edition. If it's only one or two relevant chapters then photocopy them in the library. Lesser texts can be bought second-hand at bookshops, at fairs or through notice boards in your department or academic websites, so long as they are not too outdated.

- **Equipment**
Depending on your course content, this could be anything from white lab coats to art equipment. Make sure it's all necessary. Sometimes there's a standard pack you have to buy from your department.

- **Filing**
Get into the habit of sorting out your paperwork regularly. Use different files for each module or subject, and for administration and other paperwork.

- **Resources**
Pay the library a visit, if you haven't already. You may also need to check out other resources such as design studios, language labs, computer rooms or study skills centres.

COURSE AND TERM STRUCTURE
Know when to turn up, and what gets you the most points towards your degree.

TERMS AND SEMESTERS

Some universities use a two-semester system, and others work to a three-term structure to divide up working time and holidays. At the moment these vary from university to university, but as a very rough idea:

- **There will be an autumn semester beginning approximately at the end of September and ending around the end of January, plus a spring semester starting around the beginning of February and ending mid-June. Each semester has a short break within it.**

- **OR There will be three terms, with approximate dates of end-September to mid-December, start of January to end of March, and end-April to mid-June. The terms have different names, according to the institution you're studying at.**

COURSE STRUCTURES

The average university degree will earn you the qualification of Bachelor of Arts or Science, and takes three years to complete (four in Scotland). Sandwich degrees have a year out working in industry. Someone who is studying dual (or combined) honours is taking two subjects within the same degree, rather than doing two degree courses simultaneously.

More courses are becoming modular, i.e. broken down into separate units, allowing you to choose between different areas of study. When picking modules, consider how useful they will be after you graduate, how much they interest you and how well you think you'll perform academically. If you decide you don't like a particular module, change to another as soon as possible (see notes at the end of this chapter).

MAKING THE GRADE

Know how you're being assessed and how many marks each activity is worth towards your final grade. Marks can be split between exams, continuous assessment of coursework, practical work and perhaps a final year project or dissertation. Do the most work on areas that will gain you the largest proportion of marks.

Students who do very well academically are awarded first-class degrees (or 'firsts') and may also be awarded special prizes or distinctions, and students who score slightly below this are awarded '2.1'. Below this students who score slightly less are given a '2.2', and students who score lower than this either pass their degree with a 'third' or fail the course. It's worth knowing exactly how many marks you require to get into each category and checking your marks from time to time to see if you are on track.

OVERSEAS STUDY

Part of your course may involve studying abroad, most often during the first semester of the final year. It's a big challenge, looks good on your CV and increases your opportunities for travel during the holidays. There can be heavy competition for places, and grants and other funding may be available, so if you're interested then start looking at your departmental website and ask staff as early as you can.

PEOPLE

STAFF/UNI STRUCTURE

The figurehead of the university is the chancellor, and their job is largely ceremonial. The real head honcho is the vice-chancellor. Below them in the administrative pecking order are staff such as the registrar, deans (who oversee each faculty or broad subject area), heads of department (who oversee divisions within each faculty) and support staff. The top academic people are the professors, and below them are senior lecturers, lecturers and tutors.

YOUR PERSONAL TUTOR

When you arrive at university, you are assigned a personal tutor. They are supposed to be your first port of call for any major issues to do with your general welfare or academic progress, but the relationship can be pretty variable.

LECTURERS AND TUTORS

These people are responsible for teaching, setting and marking coursework, supervising dissertations and projects, and so on. Most of them respond best to students who don't give them heaps of attitude, appear to be taking an interest in the subject and get their work in on time.

Teaching staff are an invaluable resource. Drop by their offices briefly from time to time to get your face known, or email them quick questions, and you'll start building up a useful rapport. They can lend or suggest books, saving you hours hunting them down in the library, and possibly going off on useless tangents. You can also make appointments with them to discuss essay structure, research skills or general progress, and they might tip you off about subjects that turn up in exams. Staff can eventually provide you with glowing references when you start applying for employment or help set up projects for postgraduate study.

SUPPORT STAFF

Your departmental receptionists and secretaries are your first port of call when you need to make appointments, complain about lecturers not turning up, hand in your coursework, ask about lost property or fill in any administrative forms. If you want something done, it's better to be polite and persistent, and it never hurts to pay them the occasional compliment.

COURSE MATES

The other people in your year can be a motley crew, but sometimes that's part of the fun. Even if you don't have much in common with course mates, keep on good terms with them. After all, if it's a specialised or vocational course, you may well end up working with them or bumping into them for many years to come.

Hopefully you'll end up with a happy atmosphere and a healthy amount of socialising. Some courses can have a competitive atmosphere, and occasionally students resort to dodgy tactics to get ahead of their peers, spreading gossip or 'forgetting' to tell others about important course information. It's all rather sad and childish, and smacks of insecurity, but stay positive and don't stoop to their level.

USEFUL SKILLS
Many of these skills are useful long after you have graduated, in everyday life and the world of employment.

TIME MANAGEMENT
Most students who manage their time well use a seven-day timetable, similar to their course timetable, but including the weekends and evenings. They also note everything down in their diaries, and know how to say 'no' when overloaded.

When you're making a timetable, in addition to your academic activities, include: lunch breaks, travel, clubs and meetings, exercise, part-time jobs, time with friends or partners.

MOTIVATION AND ATTITUDE
Naturally you will find some of your study topics more interesting than others. If it's a subject you find difficult you will have to work harder to gain a better understanding of it. If it's a subject you don't struggle with, but just dislike, reward yourself every time you attend a lecture or do an hour of private study. If it's the teaching that's dull, get a mate to take lecture notes for you and use the extra time to find out about the subject in another way. If you find your course dull or difficult to understand most or all of the time, this is a sign of impending trouble – you may be better off changing courses or need extra support from tutors.

NETWORKING
Get used to chatting to all kinds of people about your course or anything that inspires you, because you never know what they might come up with. You may find new tips for studying, useful book recommendations, offers of help or new contacts for work or further study. Be prepared to help others

out in return. After you leave university, you may find that contacts from your student days are invaluable in the world of work.

WRITTEN ENGLISH

No matter what your degree subject, you need good written English. Using the correct spelling, grammar and punctuation helps you to communicate your ideas in the best way possible, and it makes you look more intelligent. Spelling and grammar checkers on computers can help somewhat, but make sure you're always using the British English version. They often miss words that are incorrect for the particular sentence you're writing. For example 'their' and 'there' are commonly mixed up by some writers, but not spotted by spellcheckers. An examiner would notice it, though. The final check through has to be done by you. Buy a dictionary and use it regularly. If your course has lots of jargon invest in a subject dictionary.

Most students know if their written English is slightly shaky. If that includes you, maybe try a small book about punctuation and grammar. If you're having trouble reading and writing, and suspect you may be dyslexic, contact the Adult Dyslexia Organisation (tel: 020 7924 9559). If your first language isn't English, spend as much time with native English speakers as you can. International students may have access to free English classes. It can also help to get English friends to check your assignments before you hand them in – try bribing them with food.

Several books can help your writing skills, including *Basic Written English* by Don Schiach, John Murray, £5.99 and *Good Grammar* by Graham King, Collins, £5.99.

EXTRA CLASSES

Increasing numbers of people are arriving at university who don't enter via the traditional GCSE and A-level route. They may be offered optional or compulsory extra classes in anything from study skills to extra physics. There are often several helpful classes or short courses on offer from freshers' week onwards, which should be advertised in your welcome pack or in the students' union, the library or the computing centre.

EMAIL

Every undergraduate student should be given a university email address. You can use it when applying for work experience or doing research to prove your identity. However, computer services staff may monitor the content of emails you send and receive, so watch what you're doing and keep your dodgy dealings to personal webmail addresses. Many tutors and faculty offices use email as their main method of disseminating important information, such as timetable changes or assignment details, so check regularly for urgent messages.

WORD PROCESSING

It is rare for students to be allowed to hand in handwritten assignments. Use an easily readable simple font, and use plain white paper. Leave a decent-sized margin to allow whoever is assessing your work to make notes and comments, and use the spacing your department asks for.

BACKING UP

Always, always keep an extra copy of anything you're going to hand in for marking. Ask around any group of final-year students and there will almost certainly be a horror story of a virus chewing its way through an essay document an hour before it was due in or a computer being stolen with a final year dissertation on the hard drive. Don't assume you're fine because you're working on a Mac and 'they never crash'.

SPREADSHEETS

The more scientific your course, the more you're likely to need to use spreadsheets, so get yourself booked onto a free course if you can.

STATISTICS

Any course that expects you to conduct experiments will also require you to collect data and present the results. Statistics are mostly pretty straightforward. Doing your stats tends to fall into two main categories: descriptive and comparative. Descriptive stats get you looking at a bunch of results and finding ways to describe them as a whole.

Generally speaking, the larger the sample size the more likely it is that you've got a realistic set of results. You can also use statistics to compare groups – for example, do the science undergraduates at your university have higher IQs than the arts graduates? Try *Statistics Without Tears: An Introduction for Non-mathematicians* by Derek Rowntree, Penguin Science, £8.99.

RESEARCH

You need to know how to find and evaluate useful materials.

THE LIBRARY

The library will have an electronic catalogue of books that you can search using keywords, author or editor names, subjects or titles. The system each library uses to classify the books can vary, but books on a similar subject are usually stored close together. Catalogues also list periodicals and journals in stock.

Often-used or expensive books are reference only, so you can't take them out of the library. They may be shelved in an open reference area or you may have to sign up to use them by the hour.

When looking for periodicals and articles, they may be listed in online databases, CD-ROMs or printed catalogues. Find out how to search each of these by title, author, keyword and subject. Newspaper and magazine articles may also be kept in stock in paper form or on microfiche if they are older.

Your department probably has its own library or resource room too.

HOW TO RESEARCH

Research, evaluation and analysis, and critical thinking are all important skills that you need to do well in your degree. Here are a few tips:

- **Look through textbooks, course outline and lecture notes to get a basic overview, noting down useful references. Talk to lecturers and librarians to get ideas. Try initial internet searches.**

- Browse the library catalogue, noting relevant subject headings.

- Go through the library's reference section for anything that may be relevant, from subject-specific dictionaries to general encyclopaedias.

- Browse through preliminary material, writing brief notes on anything interesting. Jot down a plan of what to write, and the research materials needed.

- Go back to the library and search for specialist books, journal articles, etc. Read online abstracts to check articles are relevant.

- Check recent journal or magazine articles for your subject – they may not be catalogued yet.

- Get copies of work that is frequently referenced in what you're collecting, either in the main text or in bibliographies.

- You may find that useful items in the catalogue or databases are out on loan or kept in different libraries – get them on order as soon as you can. You may have to pay a small fee for the service.

- Start to evaluate the material you have collected, and be flexible. It may prompt you to do some additional research.

CRITICAL EVALUATION OF MATERIAL

It isn't enough to quote articles or books. You have to be able to summarise what the authors are saying, and evaluate their research and analysis to see if it's been correctly carried out and has logical conclusions. If you can gain these skills, you stand a much better chance of getting a first or a 2:1, whatever your subject. When reading a research article, read through the abstract, any subject headings, the results and the conclusions. This should give you an idea of whether or not the material is suitable for what you're trying to study. Then go back and briefly skim read through the whole thing to get the gist of their research, what authors are trying to prove, how they tried to prove it, what their results were and how they interpreted them. Then read through once more, in detail.

Ask yourself the following questions:

- **Are the researchers experts in their field, is the article or chapter in a well-known and respected publication, and has the work been reviewed by other respected experts before publication?**

- **Have the researchers carried out the study in a logical way? Could their results be biased due to the way they have set the study up?**

- **What theory are they trying to prove or disprove?**

- **Have they recorded measurements properly?**

- **Have they carried out correct statistical tests?**

- **When you look at the results, do conclusions they've drawn from them make sense?**

- **What other theories are they drawing upon when they make conclusions from their results?**

- **Are their arguments rational and unbiased? Have they deliberately/accidentally ignored any important information?**

When you're reading new research and information, ignore your personal beliefs, prejudices, opinions, traditions and any 'received wisdom'. See if the researchers are consistent, coherent, and if you can apply their model to real experiences. Does their argument flow well, make sense and avoid emotional appeals to the reader? You may find that some parts of their work are done well, but others have weaknesses. Being able to spot the difference is invaluable when you're writing reviews and essays. You need to compare different schools of thought and possibly argue for the one that has the most weight behind it. Try *Critical Thinking for Students: Learn the Skills of Critical Assessment and Effective Argument* by Roy Van Den Brink-Budgen, How To Books, £9.99.

INTERNET RESEARCH
The internet can be helpful for gathering information for your coursework, but isn't perfect.

- **Start by looking at your university, library or departmental website to see if they contain course information or recommend any online resources.**

- **There may be well-known online databases specific to your subject.**

- **You can also search for general background reading using search engines like www.google.com or www.ask.co.uk. Get the hang of using search engines efficiently to help narrow down the search. If you're looking for something topical, try searching websites of newspapers and broadcasters.**

Be aware that the information you're looking for may not be published online. Always consult lecture notes, textbooks, people, and other resources as well.

When you're looking at the content of a website, ask yourself a few questions:

- **Is this up-to-date information?**

- **Is this biased information? Is it written by a political group, a company who stands to make financial gain, a religious group, or cranks?**

- **What are the credentials of the author? If it's from a leading authority, such as a top academic, a regulatory body, a government research agency or a well-known journal, this has more weight.**

- **Are any facts and figures correct? Do they tally roughly with other research in the area?**

If you want to use internet material in assignments, reference it properly and include web addresses in your bibliography section, plus date accessed. Don't use huge chunks of text word for word, unless you put them inside quotation marks to show that it's not being illegally passed off as your own work.

ATTENDANCE REQUIRED

If you're going to haul yourself out of bed at some ungodly hour, you might as well make the most of your lectures, tutorials, practicals and so on.

LECTURES

Lectures are a formal method of teaching. Attend as many as you can; they're an excellent short cut to finding out the most important information for your studies and there may be essential administrative or academic announcements that you wouldn't otherwise hear about. If you can't attend a particular lecture, ask someone if you can copy his or her notes afterwards.

Asking questions is a point of etiquette – if there's a word, concept or phrase used at the beginning of the lecture that you're not familiar with, ask the lecturer what it means or how it is spelled so you can look it up later. Don't bombard the lecturer with questions throughout their talk, it disrupts the flow and annoys the audience by making the whole thing drag on. Write extra queries down and catch the staff member after they've finished.

Quality note-taking will help you with everything from research to exam revision, so get into the habit early on.

- **Note the date and the subject when you start, to help with your filing, and keep your handwriting as neat as you can.**

- **You don't have to write down everything the lecturer says, just summarise the main points. Write down quotes and references word for word.**

- **Use subheadings and bullet points to break up text as you go along, and include any recommended reading.**

- **Sometimes lecturers provide printed notes. Add your own comments to them.**

- **Some students prefer to tape lectures or use a laptop.**

Taking in lecture information is passive learning. To reinforce what you have learned, carry out active learning too. Read through notes again afterwards and add a few more comments if necessary. It may help to use coloured pens to underline or highlight key words or sentences. Work on your own initiative and check notes against other sources of information, and carry out recommended reading. When you have a good idea of the topic, make a few summary notes in your own words for quick reference later.

TUTORIALS AND SEMINARS

These are regular meetings between tutors and small groups of students. There may be teaching, discussion of theories or results, feedback on your essays or practicals, or small presentations by the students. Tutorials can be a useful environment to gain a deeper knowledge of your subject.

When you know what the subject of the tutorial is going to be, read ahead a little, and make a few brief notes to help you get the most out of it. Then try to make at least one intelligent-sounding comment during the seminar or ask one or two probing questions. Before you leave, make a note of anything you have to prepare before the next tutorial.

PRACTICALS

Most courses with vaguely scientific content will have practicals at some point, and the more scientific it is, the longer and more regular they tend to be. Students may be expected to work alone, in pairs or in groups, usually in a laboratory. You should be given a handout or booklet in advance to explain exactly what you need to do and what equipment you will need. As there is always some scientific principle or other behind it, or you're supposed to be replicating some famous experiment or learning a specific skill, it might help to read around the subject a little to see how your results are supposed to look before you start. You will be expected to provide a written report at the end of most practicals, so be prepared.

Go through instructions carefully and see if your supervisor has anything important to add before you start. Then, work out how long each step of the process should take, taking note of safety instructions. If you're working in pairs or groups, make sure everyone is doing a roughly equal amount of the work.

Take notes as you go along, in a bound notebook or the practical booklet, not on loose scraps of paper that could get lost. If there are any periods where you're waiting around, start writing up to save time later. You may be expected to hand in on the day, or later as a longer report. When you're marked for practical work and report writing, you get points for carrying out instructions properly, finishing and handing in on time, recording and presenting your results in the right format and interpreting or evaluating the results in accordance with the relevant literature.

FIELD TRIPS

This is where a group of students is sent out to see or learn something first hand, in the company of a tutor or lecturer, for a day or sometimes longer. If there is some kind of learning outcome or project work to hand in when you get back, write everything down as you go along and keep any relevant sketches or diagrams safe. Otherwise, use the trip to gain some orientation or general experience within the working environment.

ASSIGNMENTS AND EXAMS

ESSAYS

Essays can make up a significant proportion of your degree marks, so it pays to have good technique. Start researching early before somebody else takes the main texts out of the library.

To avoid some of the commonest mistakes:

- **Write down the essay question word for word, and make a careful note of the date it is due in and how many words it should be in length.**

- **Study the question, and look closely at how it is worded. For example, if it says 'discuss. . .' then you're being asked to show all sides of an** argument and give critical evaluations of them all. If it says 'outline. . . .' then you need to summarise all the important points of this specific subject, and so on.

- If the essay title mentions the names of researchers, authors or philosophers then make yourself a mini-expert on their work with some background reading before you start.

- If you don't understand the question, have a quiet word with the tutor.

- Ask about the assessment criteria for the essay and use these as a checklist.

The next step is to research your essay:

- Generally, if a journal article is cited by many other journal articles, it is probably well-known and respected. Read it critically and be certain it is up to date.

- Use a mix of classic and current research to give a sense of history and show you've thoroughly researched the subject.

- Make rough notes as you go along, and you should find that a plan for your essay starts to develop.

- Most essays have the following structure: an introduction where you outline the main points that you are about to discuss, a longer arguments section where you discuss the relevant research in the field and the differing opinions within it, a brief summary section where you evaluate the research and give your conclusions based on the evidence, and a references or bibliography section.

If you've done your research but still feel confused about what to include in your essay, get in touch with your tutor or lecturer. Ask if there are any other references you need or if they think you've missed anything out.

Once you've done your notes and planning, decide on your section headings and how long they'll be. Then start writing:

- **Keep your writing style clear and simple to show you understand the principles behind various arguments, and use correct terminology.**

- **Don't waffle.**

- **Show critical thinking, back up comments and opinions with relevant research.**

- **When quoting large passages of text or reporting speech, always use quotation marks and credit the writer/speaker.**

- **Update references section as you go – saves time later.**

Take care with presentation and lay the essay out as your department has requested, or you can lose valuable marks. Make sure your name is at the top of the paper or your student number for anonymous marking, plus the exact essay title or question. Stick to the word count, which you should mention at the start or end of the text, and lay out your references in the bibliography using the exact ordering system that your university wants you to use. When you've finished, take a break from it for a while if possible, and come back to read it through again later. Look for mistakes in spelling, grammar and punctuation, and make sure you really have answered the essay question. When you're finished, print out a good quality copy of the essay and hand it in, keeping a copy of your own.

ON CHEATING

Don't even think about using copies of other people's work and then passing it off as your own. It's plagiarism and you could even get thrown off your course. By all means look at what other students have written in previous years to see what's considered to be an excellent essay, but do your own research and thinking, and make sure it's in your own words.

REVIEWS

Writing reviews has much in common with essay writing, but rather than answering a question using quotes from a variety of sources, you're evaluating a single piece of work, e.g. a book, journal paper or television documentary. Read or watch thoroughly and write a brief description of its key points, then discuss the accuracy or validity of the research or ideas contained within it, and make your conclusions. Where possible, refer to several books, articles or other resources that evaluate the material you're reviewing. Include sources that disagree with one another, or represent a more modern branch of thought, and if the weight of argument supports one way of thinking more than the others, note this.

FINAL-YEAR DISSERTATIONS OR PROJECTS

These are long pieces of work where you're showcasing your research and analytical skills. If you have to do a dissertation, obtain departmental guidelines and find a supervisor. A good supervisor can help you choose the best area to study (with realistic limits) and use the best methods of analysis, show you how to recruit volunteers, sign your application to the ethics committee if necessary, proof-read your drafts and keep you motivated. If possible, pick a fairly narrow topic that's interesting and you can cover well.

Copies of final-year dissertations end up in your faculty office or the library, so look at a few before you start. Dissertations take the form of an extended essay, commonly eight to twelve thousand words long. A good one usually has an abstract at the beginning, where the results and conclusions are outlined briefly in a paragraph of text, and a section at the end that suggests further work that could be done as the result of carrying out the dissertation project. That's in addition to the usual introduction, a literature review, original research, discussion of the findings, plus a large bibliography.

Try *Research Survival Guide* by Ann Marttinen and R.N. Doordan, Lippincott Williams and Wilkins, £15.00 or *Research Made Real* by Mark Walsh, Nelson Thornes, £10.75.

PRESENTATIONS

Student presentations seem to cause more anxiety than any other academic activity, apart from exams. With good preparation you'll be fine.

- **Make sure you know what your topic area is, when your presentation will be and how long it lasts.**

- **Read around your subject thoroughly and decide what you want to talk about.**

- **Prepare your 'script', writing it out in full, and read it aloud while timing yourself. If it's too long or short, adjust.**

- **Include one or two jokes at the beginning or start with an interesting question, and ensure the topics flow smoothly.**

- **Try making a few cards with the main points of your talk on them, so that you can look up more at your audience when you're talking.**

- **The more you practise the less intimidating it feels.**

Then think about your voice: stand up straight when you're speaking to allow yourself to breathe properly. Take a couple of slow, measured breaths before you start. Speak up so people at the back of the room can hear. If you find yourself talking too quickly, slow yourself down by counting to four in your head after finishing each subsection, before starting on the next one. Make eye contact with the audience.

If a projector or slides will help, use them, keeping your visible text to no more than five simple lines or bullet points per page or slide, and making your diagrams look as professional as you can. Provide handouts if you like. After your conclusions or summing up, ask the audience if they have any questions.

EXAMS

Here's how to make the most of the time available, and how to cope with stress.

PREPARATION

This is essential if you want to succeed. Start by making a revision timetable, using the relevant areas of your course outline as a guide for all the topics. Make sure you can cover all of the main areas in the time you allow yourself for each topic, and leave some extra time at the end for troubleshooting. Double check with your tutor and departmental office about subjects and formats of exams, and how long each lasts. Will you be writing essays, or long or short answer questions, or will it all be multiple choice? Ask for past papers, for an idea of the questions they'll ask, plus the correct answers.

REVISING

Start by skim-reading through your notes to refresh your memory, then read them through again more thoroughly a couple of times to make sure you understand them properly. If you haven't done so already, start to make brief summaries of the most important points. Some students like to use file cards for this because they are a convenient size. Don't put too much on one card, keep it simple, and feel free to use colour coding or diagrams if they help to make more of an impact. Keep looking at summary notes or cards to memorise them.

You can also make up mnemonics to help you to remember more complex sequences of facts. These are phrases or funny rhymes, where each word or letter corresponds to each fact you need to remember. Different people respond to different modes of learning, so you may need to gear your revision to words you can read, diagrams or images you can look at, or recordings that you can listen to. Experiment to see what works for you.

Test yourself after your day's work. You can write your own questions, use past papers or look new ones up online. Find areas where you need to improve your memory or understanding. Your timetable may include exam technique tutorials or mock papers.

Last-minute revision is not the best way to learn, but all is not lost. Prioritise the most important subject areas and skim through notes and textbooks for the remaining information. Hopefully you'll know much of it already. Try not to read too much unfamiliar material late at night or in the morning before an exam – you probably won't remember and it makes it harder to recall other information you've recently learned.

EXAM STRESS

There are several practical ways to reduce your stress levels before exams.

- **Take short regular breaks.**

- **Bigger breaks such as an occasional meal with friends, or a trip to the cinema, are good too.**

- **If you have revised well and stuck to your timetable, give yourself rewards.**

- **Eat regular balanced meals.**

- **Get to bed at a reasonable time, avoid coffee or strong tea late at night.**

- **Take regular exercise.**

Student welfare services help students suffering from exam stress, offering counselling or relaxation classes. If you're feeling sick with worry, see your GP.

The night before the exam, avoid last-minute revision of new material if at all possible, and pack your bag with everything you need. Set out some comfortable clothes. In the morning, get up in plenty of time to eat breakfast and make your way to the exam without rushing.

THE EXAM

When you arrive at the exam hall, it's normal to feel a rush of adrenaline. A little nervous tension improves performance. Take a couple of long, slow breaths and tell yourself that you probably know a lot more than you think you do right now!

- **Read instructions slowly and carefully.**

- **If you have a choice of questions, make sure you know how many you need to do in total.**

- **Make a plan: divide up your time between the questions, allowing extra time for ones that are worth more marks.**

- **Allow time at the end for checking.**

If you're doing essays, write a short plan at the start of each answer. Include brief notes on the main points examiners will look for. Use neat handwriting and stick to your plan, checking that you're answering the question that has been asked. Move on to the next question if you run out of time. If your paper consists of short or long answer questions, stick to key concepts or 'buzz words' in your answers. If you feel stuck, move on to questions you can answer and go back later.

Multiple-choice papers have several similar possible answers for each question; cover up the possible answers while you read the question first to avoid confusion. The correct answer will hopefully pop into your head and then you can read through the options to see which is the closest. Watch out for ambiguous language among the possible answers. Make sure you know if your department is using negative marking (where points are deducted for each wrong answer) or not. If they aren't, make a guess at all questions you're not sure about.

IF YOU'RE FEELING PANICKY DURING AN EXAM, TRY THESE TIPS:

- **Take a long, slow, deep breath, hold for a count of three, then slowly exhale. Repeat this a couple of times and you should start to feel a little bit calmer.**

- **Concentrate your attention on something else to take your mind off panicky thoughts. Try focusing on the pen you're holding, or the view out of the window.**

MISSING EXAMS

If you think you will be unable to take one or all of your exams, let the university know straight away. Get a medical certificate, if needed.

EXAM AFTERMATH

When an exam is over, unwind. Avoid exam post-mortems where people discuss the paper or say they've failed.

When the results come back, if you scored much lower than you expected, speak to a tutor immediately. Occasionally marks are added up wrongly, but if you've ruled that out then face up to your mistakes and learn from them. Improve study or exam technique and do resits, or make points up by getting better marks for attendance, essays and projects. If you got the grades you were aiming for, congratulations!

HAVING PROBLEMS?

CHANGING COURSE

It's common to wonder if you're doing the right course, especially at the beginning of your first year. Most students go through phases of feeling like this. However, you may decide you genuinely dislike the university or your course.

Generally, if you're taking the wrong subject, the course content feels completely uninspiring or you struggle to get your head around any of it. The course might also be in the wrong format for you. Perhaps you're currently doing a module you hate.

When you've decided exactly what you dislike, find something positive to replace it. Do you want to stay where you are but change course modules, change location or subject, or is university just not for you? Don't bump along becoming demotivated or drop out without explanation. Talk to someone about it, such as your personal tutor, trusted friends or reasonable relatives.

If you want to stay within the university system, find alternative courses. Find out if there are places available this year or next, and whether they will take you on. UCAS is a good place to start, and your personal tutor may also make suggestions or make calls on your behalf. Phone tutors on prospective courses. If you find what you're looking for, contact your local education authority to see if you can rearrange funding. The earlier you change, the more likely they'll be able to help. After this, see your head of department to find out about course transfer rules or forms you need to fill in. When you start the new course there will be lots of catching up to do, and it may be easier to start again the following academic year.

FALLING BEHIND WITH WORK

If you're late with assignments, not doing your self-directed study and your attendance is poor, you aren't going to get good grades.

The main cause of falling behind is simply being disorganised. If this sounds like you, take a good look at your timetable and motivate yourself to get on with what you need to do. Maybe your part-time job is eating into your study time or you don't go to the library enough. You may have to make unpleasant decisions that mean less money or less time with your mates or loved ones. Allow enough extra study time for catching up.

If you are struggling with the work itself, rather than the time you've allowed for it, speak to a tutor urgently. Universities are more sympathetic to students who ask for help before they start failing their subjects, rather than afterwards.

PROBLEMS WITH ACADEMIC STAFF

Under the students' charter, you are entitled to expect a minimum standard of teaching and general conduct from staff. It's natural for certain students not to get on with certain lecturers, simply because of personality clashes. Don't push your luck, and remember a little politeness and respect goes a long way.

If you are being subjected to abusive comments, they're not turning up to teach or your essays go unmarked, you have grounds for complaint. Keep a note of what's happened, what was said and how long it has been going on for. If it's an issue that's affecting all or most of your year group, make a joint complaint. Raise concerns via a senior member of your department, personal tutor or NUS representative.

If you think a member of staff has singled you out for unfair treatment because of your gender, race, sexuality or religion keep a record of prejudiced remarks and get witnesses to come forward. Several organisations can advise, from the LGBSoc officer to the Campaign for Racial Equality (see Contacts).

Sexual harassment from staff is occasionally a problem, and may be subtle or overt. Many institutions also have strict rules banning staff from dating their students. Don't put up with any behaviour that makes you uncomfortable, tell anyone who is behaving inappropriately that their actions are unwelcome, avoid being left alone with that person wherever possible and get some moral support while you make a complaint.

DISABILITY

One in ten of us has some form of disability, and most university staff are more than willing to give their students some extra support. Wherever possible, remind the university well ahead of time that you're likely to need things such as improved physical access, permission to tape lectures and so on. Contact SKILL, the national bureau for students with disabilities (see Contacts).

CHAPTER 4: HEDONISM

University is an all-round experience, and no way are you supposed to spend every night studying on your own. Meet, greet, snog, be entertained and expand your horizons.

This chapter looks at:

- **Entertainment: what's on offer, making your own**
- **Sex and dating: chatting up, relationships, sexual health**
- **Alcohol: cheap drinking, hangovers, safety tips**
- **Drugs: laws, effects, first aid**

HEDONISM ON A BUDGET
You can have a rich social life, but you have to make compromises. Make your money stretch further by developing good blagging skills:

- **Be charming and friendly.**
- **Be cheeky. Invite yourself to parties.**
- **Always ask for money off. Flash your NUS card.**
- **Offer to help out.**
- **Work your contacts.**

ENTERTAIN US

STATE OF THE UNION
Most students' union buildings lay on a wide range of events all year round, mostly at low prices. Expect live music, comedy, club nights, big screen

sport, themed parties, karaoke or cinema. Clubs and societies may also host events. Look out for posters and flyers in the union building.

YOU'VE GOT BALLS

Balls or formals happen once or twice a year, so they're big blowouts. If you're lucky they're held in a classy venue and include a decent meal. Many students hire or borrow their outfits for the evening; there's no need to buy a pricey 'black tie' outfit or ball gown you'll never use again.

RAG WEEK

These are fundraising weeks full of strange and silly activities for charity, organised by the university's RAG team. Get involved yourself or sponsor mates.

A NIGHT ON THE TOWN

Many clubs do cheap student nights with drink offers, and there's something for most musical tastes. Ask for student discount wherever you go; a wide range of restaurants, cinemas and theatres have at least one night of the week where they are cheaper. Afternoon showings of films and plays tend to be cheaper at the start of the week. Most cinema chains have student areas on their websites containing special deals, email newsletters, competitions and complimentary advance screening tickets. Students may get free entry to some art and historical exhibitions too.

GETTING INVOLVED

If you want to be invited to more parties, meet bands or get on guest lists, do some work in the entertainment field. Train up to do sound or lighting for student union events, lug band equipment from van to stage or be responsible for booking the acts. Or you can project films, sell tickets on the door, work in a pub or club or be an usher or wardrobe assistant in the local theatre. If you're more of an extrovert, form a band or DJ. Some students arrange their own club nights or other events.

FESTIVAL SEASON

The long summer holidays make it easy to get to most of the British music and arts festivals. If you're driving down, set off early to avoid traffic jams.

Camping out tips:

- Don't take anything expensive to a festival, including fancy tents. Keep cameras etc. with you.

- Arrive early and find a good spot.

- Arrange a meeting point in advance with your friends. Remember that mobile phone reception can be poor.

- Make your tent easy to find. Tie a balloon or flag to it.

- Decide what bands you want to see, but be flexible.

- Expect to pay extra for food, drink and other items on site. Have some munchies in your bag when you arrive.

- The toilets will be disgusting. If possible, get up early and use them in the morning after cleaning.

- Think twice before buying drugs from dealers at festivals.

- Plan for all kinds of weather. Take waterproofs, warm clothes and wellies or plastic bags to tie around your shoes. Also bring light clothing, sunscreen, sunglasses and a hat.

- Useful items: small rucksack, water, loo roll, matches, torch, penknife, painkillers, condoms, plasters, wet wipes and something to sit on.

- If you're having difficulties, go to festival stewards, first aid facilities or the Samaritans tent.

DIY ENTERTAINMENT

Sometimes you have to make your own amusement. It's the perfect way to see your friends without spending a fortune and it's much better than staying home alone feeling sorry for yourself when you're skint. Throw a house party or a dinner party, turn up to someone else's or arrange a cheap evening in or out.

HOUSE PARTIES

Pick a night all your flatmates agree on, decide how many people you want to invite and think about security issues.

Before the night of your party, speak to your neighbours to warn them what you're planning. Clear away breakables or expensive items. Clear out fridge, kitchen cupboards, living room, bathroom – if it isn't nailed down, someone will nick it or have a food fight. Think about fire exits and clear corridors.

Get as many ashtrays as you can and put out big bins for the empty bottles and cans. Sort out your lighting, but avoid candles: they can easily get knocked over by passing drunks. Decide what's happening with the music – make time slots for people to DJ so they're not fighting over the decks or make a big playlist of MP3s or burned CDs (then hide your music collection).

Fix up drinks and snacks. Make sure guests know they'll need to bring some alcohol too. Get beer chilling in the fridge or use a bath full of cold water if you need more cooling space. If you're making cocktails, stick to just one or two simple recipes so you don't need to buy too many ingredients.

Have plastic cups for when you run out of glasses. Corkscrews and bottle openers have a habit of getting lost at house parties – tie them onto a long piece of string attached to a cupboard door handle. Put crisps or tortilla chips out to soak up the booze.

Guests tend to arrive as the pubs close, so pace yourself. If possible, bribe someone beefy to be the door person, keeping out unwanted gatecrashers. After that, just relax and enjoy. If your party goes well, you will be the party king or queen and the envy of your friends for the rest of term.

When the party's over, most people get the message and clear off home. If they don't, play terrible music, turn the lights on and tell them to sod off, or rope them into Operation Clean-up:

- Get someone to walk around the whole place once or twice during the evening with a bin bag collecting empty bottles and cans to keep the mess down.

- Keep a mess kit handy: rubber gloves, paper towels, wiping-up cloths, cleaning fluid, carpet stain remover, plastic bags and air freshener (see cleaning tips in Appendix).

- Have a quick run round the house after the party and collect empty glasses, leftover food, ashtrays etc. Make sure there are no cigarette stubs still burning.

DINNER PARTIES

Invite a set number of guests and make sure you have enough chairs and plates. Choose simple recipes that you can make in bulk and if in doubt make something vegetarian, it's cheaper and just about everyone will be able to eat it. Try making big pies, stews, curries, bakes or casseroles. If you only have a small oven, don't serve three hot courses. Ask your guests to bring starters, nibbles, puddings or wine to keep the costs down and to get everyone involved.

PAUPERS' NIGHTS

Even when you're broke, you can still have a social life. Get friends round for a big bowl of pasta in front of your favourite TV show or have a film night where you all chip in to hire a couple of DVDs. Squeeze as many people onto the sofa as you can and sit the rest on some floor cushions. Ask around to see if anyone has a games console, board games or a couple of packs of cards, and arrange a games night. If you want a night on the town, find out if anywhere nearby needs a rent-a-crowd, for free entry and a free drink. Attend a gallery opening, or a free gig in a music store.

TRAVEL

The world is your oyster, even if you aren't loaded. Snap up last-minute package deals, travel independently on a shoestring or fit some local exploring in around working holidays or international exchange placements.

Or maybe a friend's relative owns holiday property abroad and all you'll have to do is pay for your transport and pocket money if you get an invite.

- **Think about all of the places you'd like to visit. Talk to people who've already been there or ask for other recommendations. Make a hit list.**

- **Borrow travel books and use travel websites to find out more about budget travel and special events in these countries, swap tips on message boards with other travellers.**

- **Save up as much as you can.**

- **Ring travel agents or compare prices online. STA Travel specialise in travel for students.**

- **Sort out vaccinations, visas and insurance long before you go.**

- **Check with the Home Office about political hotspots to avoid.**

- **Get yourself a youth discount card such as an ISIC card or a Euro<26 card for discounts on cultural and sporting events, and cheaper accommodation at some hostels.**

When you're travelling:

- **Have the time of your life and make new friends. Don't be scared to go a little off the tourist trail.**

- **Keep emergency numbers for health, insurance, next of kin and the nearest British embassy to hand. Have a photocopy of your passport with you in case the real one is stolen.**

- **Keep a diary, an internet blog or take photos to remind you of your travels.**

- **Make an attempt to speak the local language and respect the traditions of the country you're in.**

- **Keep in touch regularly with friends and relatives over email or the occasional phone call.**

You don't have to go outside Britain every time though. It's good to get out of town every now and again to visit friends within the UK at weekends, go to festivals, go hiking and admire some beautiful scenery or do a few touristy things closer to home. Recommended reading includes *The Virgin Travellers' Handbook* by Tom Griffiths, Virgin Books, £14.99.

SHOPPING

Books, films and music can all be bought at discount from big stores that have student days or other deals. Enter competitions, share things with friends or take out CDs, DVDs and novels from the local library for free or for a few pence. Downloading most films and MP3 music files is illegal for copyright reasons, but very few prosecutions take place.

The NUS have special deals with certain music, food and clothing chains, so check what's currently on offer before you hit the high street. If you want new clothes, buy them in the sales, as seconds or samples, or from discount stores. If there's something special you want, it might have to be a birthday or Christmas present from a kindly relative.

SEX AND DATING

Your years at university give you the easiest opportunity ever to meet attractive people and chat them up. Don't believe me? The union bar, all the entertainments, your course, clubs and societies, charity fundraising activities, bookshops, supermarkets near campus and even the university library can be right for romance. Honest. There are blind date events as part of some union entertainments programmes, free university-based romance and friendship websites and speed-dating evenings if you're a bit backwards in coming forwards.

CHATTING UP

Got your eye on someone? Get in there before someone else does. Look at someone who's skilled at it, the person who gets all the girls or all the boys, and you may find they *aren't* the best-looking person in the room. They're confident, and they've practised their pulling technique. If you don't have confidence, you can increase it or fake it. Practise generally being friendly, and make an effort to smile and make more eye contact with people. If you have chosen a target for your affections, try not to calm your nerves too much with drink. Try this instead:

- Check them out from afar by making brief eye contact and smiling, then looking away. Repeat a few times. Don't stare at them scarily all night.

- If anyone knows your 'target' already, get them to introduce you. Subtly. 'My mate fancies you' is the kiss of death.

- Be brave. If they've been holding your gaze and smiling back, go over and start talking to them.

- Ask an open question (something that needs more than a 'yes' or 'no' answer); introduce yourself and ask them their name, or pay them a compliment about something they're wearing.

- Chat-up lines never work unless they fancy you already.

- To keep the conversation flowing, ask them a few questions about themselves.

- Try to find things that you have in common.

- While you're talking, think about your body language. Keep up the eye contact and move in slightly closer. If they move back or keep looking away, back off a bit. It's generally a good sign if they move in closer, touch you lightly and mirror your posture.

- If things are going well, suggest meeting up at a particular time to have coffee or go to something you both like. Swap phone numbers or email addresses.

- If it didn't go so well, keep it light hearted or you'll look like a bad loser. Their loss anyway.

THEY SAID YES, NOW WHAT?

Call them when you said you were going to call them and play it slightly cool to begin with. If you're nervous you can go for the safe option and meet up somewhere low key like a café during the day. Or you can go for the thrill-seeker's option: an action movie, a theme park with big rides or the local aquarium's shark tank. Get to know them better, talk about your interests, flirt like crazy and hope for the best. If they're flirting back then that's great, but think before you move in for a big snog. Sometimes people give out mixed messages when they just want to be friends, and even the best of us can read the signs wrongly on occasion.

DINNER AT MY PLACE?

Cooking someone dinner is a tried and trusted student seduction technique. If they accept your invitation, double check to see if they have any special dietary requirements such as vegetarian food or a violent nut allergy. If you aren't much of a cook, find a decent recipe and practise cooking it or ask a foodie friend for help choosing or cooking the meal. Go for two well-presented courses (starter and main or main and dessert) followed by coffee. Don't make the meal too rich or fatty because indigestion is about as unsexy as it gets. If in doubt, go for something simple using good quality fresh ingredients. Pick up some wine that costs more than £2.99 per bottle for once.

Set the scene by kicking out your flatmates (bribe them if necessary), then finding matching glassware, crockery and cutlery, and fixing up some music and low lighting. You might get lucky after dinner, so straighten out your bedroom and put your best pants on too. The idea is to look as though you're incredibly sophisticated and can throw a meal together out of almost nothing, so do most of the cooking before your guest arrives and then tidy everything away. Add the finishing touches calmly in front of them. Hand them a drink and make some chit-chat while the dinner cooks, and keep the conversation flowing during the meal. Don't be too precious about your cooking – if it ends up burnt, laugh it off and ring up for a takeaway.

GETTING IT ON

Yes, yes, yes! Time to get sexy. This is the right time to point out that sex is not compulsory, no matter how it may seem. It's only for consenting adults who both feel that the time is right to get physical with one another. There may be pressures such as wanting to be like your mates, doing it to stop someone from dumping you or being desperate to lose your virginity, but frankly they are all pretty stupid reasons. Only have sex if you both want to. In fact, it never hurts to ask the other person if it's what they really want to do, especially if drink or drugs have been consumed earlier.

Quick reality check: sex with a new partner can be incredibly nerve-wracking and exciting, but it's not like the movies. Most couples find it takes a while to feel relaxed and work out what feels good, and what their partner likes. Try not to have your expectations too high at the beginning. Also, it's unrealistic to expect your partner to be psychic; sometimes you have to ask for what you want, or ask them what they're in the mood for. While you're talking, someone should bring up the subject of safer sex, preferably while you still have your underwear on. If someone isn't mature enough to talk about safer sex then they aren't mature enough to be having sex, full stop. Use condoms with a new partner for safety and peace of mind. Keep your condoms within easy reach by your bed or carry them with you.

If you have a roommate, getting a new girlfriend or boyfriend can be tricky. Come to an agreement at the start of term about having privacy if one of you gets lucky. Stick a 'do not disturb' sign on the door, send them a text message in 'code' or whatever it takes.

ONE-NIGHT STANDS

These can be anything from a horny sexual adventure to a drink-fuelled disappointment. If you're not in a committed relationship there's nothing to stop you having a night of passion if that's what you want. We aren't living in the Dark Ages any more, so if you're both completely up for it then play safely and have a good time. If you pick somebody up in a club or pub, make sure they're over the age of consent. Also remember that your partner has every right to change their mind about having sex at any point and you need to respect that completely. Tell a friend where you're going, rather than disappearing off and worrying your mates.

The morning after can be very awkward, especially if you can't remember their name or only one of you wants to get together again. Whether you make a silent getaway or not is up to you, and largely depends on how unattractive they are while they're snoring. The decent thing is to wake them up and say thanks for a great evening, but you have to go now. If you're both awake, and you have no intention of seeing them ever again, don't give them your phone number and pretend you'd like to meet up sometime.

SEXUALITY AND EXPERIMENTING

It's quite common for students to wait until they have moved away to university before coming out as gay or bisexual. They can benefit from support from the Lesbian, Gay and Bisexual Society and its welfare officer, having a few more open-minded people around or a large local gay scene. If you're thinking about coming out, there's no need to rush and you don't have to announce it to the whole world at the top of your lungs, unless that's your personal style. You may prefer to start by talking it through with a helpline such as your local LGB switchboard, or telling one sensible and trustworthy mate, then taking things from there at your own pace.

Uncertainty about sexual preferences is more widespread than you might think. Don't be in too much of a hurry to stick a label on yourself until you're absolutely sure. It may help to talk it through with a counsellor in complete confidence.

It goes without saying that the university years are a time when all kinds of people are exploring their sexuality and experimenting. A consensual one-off snog or fondle with someone doesn't define your sexual identity, unless you have a 'eureka!' moment and realise that it's the kind of sex that you prefer. On the same note, if a particular sexual activity doesn't appeal to you, then this doesn't make you a boring old prude. You don't have to do anything to impress others.

COUPLED UP

Many long-term relationships that start during university end up with people moving in together, having kids or getting married. So long as you both make an effort to see your other friends and keep up individual interests, you're not likely to miss out on the social life.

Leaving home and doing a degree can broaden your horizons, and it considerably changes many people. A long-distance relationship with somebody from your hometown may well feel the strain, especially if they stay based at home and don't go to college themselves. Your feelings for each other could become platonic, or either one of you could meet someone else instead. There's no accounting for chemistry.

BREAKING UP

Not every relationship is going to last forever, and if you're not happy with the way things are going then it's best to get this out in the open. There's no point in keeping someone hanging on if you don't feel crazy about them, and there's no point putting up with someone who doesn't treat you properly. The worst way to break up with someone is by insulting them, telling them in public that they're dumped or by being gutless and hiding behind a friend or a text message or email. It's usually easiest in the long run if you tell them face to face (or over the phone if it's a long-distance relationship) that things simply aren't working out and you want to finish the relationship. You don't have to stick the boot in or be spiteful; you may even be able to stay friends.

Break-ups may feel devastating even if they are civilised, or you may feel relief. There's no harm in taking it easy for a few days, or letting your mates come round to cheer you up. Have a good cry if you want to, or get it off your chest with someone who's a good listener. Put photographs and souvenirs away and go out and try to enjoy yourself. It takes a while to get over a bad break-up, especially if it was a long or intense relationship, but it does get easier with time.

COULD YOU BE PREGNANT?

No method of contraception is 100 per cent perfect and accidents can happen. If you're worried about being pregnant, buy a pregnancy test from a chemist or see your doctor for free testing. The latest over-the-counter test kits are accurate from the first day that your period is due. There may be no signs that you are pregnant or there may be any of the following: tiredness, increased need to pass urine, missed period, breast tingling or soreness.

If you do find you're pregnant, your legal options are to continue with the pregnancy and raise the baby yourself, give the baby up for adoption or to terminate the pregnancy (provided certain conditions are met). This can be an incredibly difficult decision and you could benefit from some unbiased counselling.

CONTRACEPTION

For anyone who's having heterosexual sex, contraception is essential if you want to avoid pregnancy. Many clinics suggest using condoms plus another method (such as the combined pill) to be doubly safe and to avoid sexually transmitted infections. Your main options are:

- *Condoms*: Sheaths made of latex or polyurethane that cover the penis during sex. Must be rolled on carefully when the penis is erect and before the penis touches the other person's body. Can be damaged by sharp nails or jewellery, or anything oil-based such as hand cream or petroleum jelly (e.g. Vaseline). There is also a female condom that can be worn inside the vagina. Condoms are the only contraceptives that also protect against most sexually transmitted infections. Easily available from chemists and supermarkets, or free from health centres and family planning clinics.

- *Combined contraceptive pill*: Pills containing oestrogen and progestogens that prevent the female body from releasing eggs. Most brands are taken daily for 21 days, followed by a 7-day break. Sometimes prescribed for painful periods or acne. Not suitable for smokers. May be made ineffective by vomiting or diarrhoea; use additional contraception such as condoms until you're protected again (usually takes five days, but check the instructions in your pill packet).

- ***Progestogen-only pill (POP):*** Pills containing progestogens. Must be taken at exactly the same time every day to be most effective. May be made ineffective by vomiting or diarrhoea.

- ***Contraceptive injection or implant:*** Contraceptive hormones that are injected into the female body or placed surgically under the skin. Useful for women who can't take the combined pill or who keep forgetting to take their pills regularly. Can cause irregular bleeding.

- ***Intra-uterine device (IUD or coil):*** Most IUDs are only suitable for women who have already had children. They are devices placed inside the womb to prevent eggs from implanting and causing pregnancy. Can be effective for up to five years.

- ***Cap or diaphragm:*** A barrier placed inside the vagina to prevent sperm reaching the cervix (the neck of the womb). Used with spermicide for extra protection. Inserted before sex and left in place for several hours afterwards.

- ***Natural methods:*** The woman carefully measures natural changes, such as variation in her body temperature, to work out the days she is most fertile. Complicated methods, only suitable for highly organised women with supportive partners.

EMERGENCY CONTRACEPTION

If you've had unprotected sex in the last five days, you may still be able to get emergency contraception, provided you get to a doctor or family planning clinic quickly. The post- coital pill (sometimes called the 'morning after' pill) is effective up to 72 hours after unprotected sex, but the sooner it is taken the more effective it is. Can be prescribed free by GPs or family planning clinics, or bought over the counter at certain chemists. Follow instructions carefully, and if you have sickness or diarrhoea after taking them, speak to the doctor/chemist to see if you need to take more. An IUD can also be inserted up to five days after having sex. Both methods prevent eggs from implanting in the womb, rather than causing abortion.

GPs and Brook Advisory Service (see Contacts) can supply more information.

SEXUALLY TRANSMITTED INFECTIONS (STIs)

You don't exist in some kind of protective bubble while you're at college; if you're sexually active you're at risk of catching sexually transmitted infections, no matter how healthy or 'nice' your partner looks. About 10 per cent of young people are currently carrying an STI – it's often impossible to tell who has one as they may have no symptoms. Although many infections can be cleared up with antibiotics, there's currently no cure for herpes and HIV, and if certain bacterial infections go undetected for long enough they can cause serious health problems.

There are three ways to reduce your risk of exposure: total abstinence, monogamy (both partners are faithful to one another and are certain they're disease free) or practising safer sex and using condoms with every partner.

Some STIs to be aware of:

- *Chlamydia*: Common bacterial infection passed on during vaginal, anal or oral sex. Women often have no symptoms, but there may be vaginal discharge, painful urination, pain during sex, irregular periods or bleeding between periods. Men may have no symptoms, or discharge from penis or burning sensation when urinating (peeing). Treated with antibiotics. If untreated, can leave women infertile.

- *Genital herpes*: Common viral infection. Passed on during anal and vaginal sex. The similar cold sore virus can also be passed on to the genitals. After infection there may be flulike symptoms and blisters around anus or genitals. Blisters burst to leave painful infectious sores taking up to four weeks to heal. There may be pain when passing urine. There may be further milder attacks later. There is no cure, but medicines help shorten the attacks.

- *Genital warts*: Viral infection spread by skin contact during vaginal or anal sex. Can cause small pinkish lumps or cauliflower-shaped lumps on penis, scrotum, anus, vulva or vagina, or flat invisible infected areas. Removed at the clinic with special paint, freezing or laser treatment. Never treat them yourself. Possibly linked to cervical cancer, so regular smear tests are important.

- *Gonorrhoea*: Common bacterial infection, passed on during oral, vaginal or anal sex. There may be no symptoms but women can have a yellowish or greenish strong smelling discharge or pain when urinating. Men can have yellow or white discharge from the penis or inflammation of testicles or prostate gland. Either sex may have irritation or discharge from the anus, or sore throat. Treatment is with antibiotics. If untreated, women can develop fever, pelvic pain, infertility.

- *Hepatitis B and C*: Viral infections passed on during sex or by sharing needles. They affect the liver and there is no known cure, but in some people the body can fight it off. May cause fever, stomach upsets, weight loss and yellowing of the skin and eyes (jaundice). If the disease progresses, there may be liver damage such as cirrhosis.

- *HIV*: Viral infection that can be passed on during anal, vaginal or oral sex, by sharing needles, or from pregnant mother to baby in the womb or in breast milk, or unchecked blood transfusions. Relatively uncommon in the UK, but increasing among the straight community. HIV (human immunodeficiency virus) weakens the body's immune system so it can't fight off infections. Eventually it can cause acquired immunodeficiency syndrome or AIDS. There is no cure for HIV, but treatments can delay onset of AIDS.

- *NSU*: A condition that affects men, usually caused by bacteria such as chlamydia. Full name: non-specific urethritis. There is burning or stinging when passing urine or discharge from penis. Treated with antibiotics.

- *Pubic (or 'crab') lice*: Tiny parasites that attach to body hair, especially in the groin. Passed on during sex or by sharing infected bedlinen or towels. Cause itching. Treated with special shampoo or lotion.

- *Scabies*: Tiny mites that burrow into the skin, causing an itchy rash, sometimes around the genitals. Passed on by close contact such as sharing a bed, or during sex. Treated with special lotion or cream.

- *Syphilis*: Bacterial infection passed on during vaginal, oral or anal sex, or from direct contact with sores. Initial infection causes painless sores (chancres) in the genital area. If left untreated, these can be followed by flu-like illness, mouth ulcers, a rash or warty growths on the genitals. It then appears to vanish, but may silently attack the body for many years, causing brain damage, heart damage or miscarriage. Treated with antibiotics.

- *Trichomonas*: Tiny parasite passed on during sex, or rarely by sharing wet towels etc. Often no symptoms, but may cause genital discharge or pain when passing urine or during sex. Treated with antibiotics.

If you suspect you might have a sexually transmitted infection, get it checked out right away. Don't hang around hoping it will disappear on its own – it might seem to have healed up but you could still be carrying the infection. You can visit your GP, or go to the nearest GUM (genito-urinary medicine) or sexual health clinic. The number for the GUM clinic will be in your local phone book, treatment's free and 100 per cent confidential.

If the clinic prescribes you some antibiotics, you must finish the course, otherwise the infection could come back. Abstain from sex until the clinic gives you the all clear, and tell your partner so they can be tested too.

OTHER COMMON SEXUAL PROBLEMS:

- *Thrush*: This is an infection caused by a yeast, *Candida albicans*. Lives naturally on human skin, but certain conditions allow it to overgrow, causing symptoms. Can be passed on to a partner during sex. In women, thrush causes itching, sore vagina and vulva, and whitish lumpy discharge. It's treated with pessaries (special tablets placed into the vagina) and cream, or oral tablets, from the chemist. Men may have itching, redness or discharge on the head of the penis, and can be treated with thrush cream. Anyone who has repeated thrush infections should go to their doctor.

- *Cystitis*: Bladder infection that mainly affects women, where there is pain when passing urine, and sometimes cloudy or dark urine, back pain, and a need to pass urine more frequently. Can be caused by bacteria from the bowel or friction from sex. During an attack, it helps to drink lots of water to flush out the bladder, and take painkillers. If the symptoms last longer than a day or two or there is blood in the urine, see a GP. Men who get cystitis should always seek medical attention.

- *Loss of libido*: Levels of desire naturally increase and decrease over time, so there's no need to worry if you have periods where you don't feel horny at all. If it goes on for weeks or months then get yourself checked out by your GP to rule out depression, stress and hormone disturbances.

- *Erectile dysfunction*: This is where a man can't get, or keep, an erection. Can happen to any man, often after too much alcohol, or stress. The stress can be anxiety about performing well sexually, or from arguing with a partner, or exam or money worries. Most of the time it's nothing to be concerned about, but a quick check-up to rule out physical illness is advised if it continues. Counselling can be effective for reducing psychological stresses.

- *Premature ejaculation*: PE or 'cumming too quickly' affects more than 10 per cent of younger men. It tends to improve with age and experience, and the man can learn distraction techniques or other methods to help him last longer. Sometimes using thicker condoms or condoms that contain a desensitising gel may do the trick. If that doesn't work, there are treatments a doctor can prescribe.

ALCOHOL

Drink can be friend or foe, depending on the circumstances. Be the boss of your own boozing.

CHEAP DRINKING

It's all about getting value for money when you're drinking at home or going out. The union bar always has cheap beer, plus regular promotions. Generally, the most cost-effective drinks are draft beer and cider, followed by wine. Hunt down cheaper pubs and clubs that are student-friendly.

Drinking at home and at parties tends to cost less, especially if you buy supermarket beers and wines in bulk with friends. Ask a relative to buy a supermarket plonk guide for you as a Christmas gift.

PACING YOURSELF

Many students pride themselves on their ability to hold their drink without falling over or vomiting. You don't have to be a hardened drinker to do this. For example:

- **Let the hard drinkers have a head start. Join them later in the evening.**

- **Eat something a while before you go out to line your stomach.**

- **Don't buy rounds. Drink at your own pace.**

- **Drink the occasional pint of water during the evening to slow down your drinking.**

- **Spirits, alcopops and cocktails are often stronger than you think. Drink slowly or stick to beer.**

Government guidelines suggest that men drink no more than 28 units of alcohol per week and that women have no more than 21 units per week, although some doctors think this is too high. One unit of alcohol is half a pint of ordinary-strength beer or cider, a small glass of wine or single measure of spirits. A standard bottle of alcopop contains one-and-a-half units.

DRUNKEN BEHAVIOUR

Being drunk can seriously affect your judgement. Exercise a little common sense. Don't let your friends walk home alone drunk at night, drink drive or get into a car with a drunk driver. Alcohol can cause you to forget to use a condom. It can also make you a target for physical or sexual assault, or make mild-mannered people become violent and aggressive. Pissed pranks such as stealing road signs and emergency lighting from roadworks, or defacing portraits or statues of your university's founder may seem hilarious at the time, but they might come back to haunt you later.

HANGOVERS

Following the 'pacing yourself' tips above can seriously reduce your risk of getting a hangover, but you might still be unlucky. Hangovers are a mixture of dehydration, the effects of toxins and low blood sugar. Get your fluids back up by drinking flat cola, isotonic sports drinks or diluted fruit juice, take a couple of painkillers and hope for the best.

ALCOHOL POISONING

Alcohol is a drug that depresses the functions of the nervous system and in large amounts it acts as a poison. Many students are hospitalised due to alcohol poisoning every year, and a few of them die or suffer permanent brain damage. Poisoning often follows a sudden bout of binge-drinking, where too much alcohol is consumed too fast. Look out for your friends. The signs of alcohol poisoning include:

- **Confusion and aggressiveness, or unconsciousness**

- **Vomiting**

- **Fits (seizures)**

- **Slow or irregular breathing**

- **Low body temperature, bluish or pale skin**

If you think someone might have alcohol poisoning, don't put them to bed to sleep it off. They could choke on their own vomit or die because of hypothermia, irregular heartbeat or suppressed breathing. While they are unconscious, their blood alcohol can continue to rise due to drink that's still in their stomach. Don't offer them coffee or get them to walk around, these make things worse. Don't try to handle an aggressive person on your own either, stay with them if you can but get some help. If you're worried about the possibility of someone having alcohol poisoning, be safe rather than sorry and call 999 for an ambulance.

SPIKED DRINKS

It's essential for both male and female students to be aware of spiked drinks. They have been used to assist robbery and sexual assault, and in some cases the attackers are fellow students. Attackers may be alone or working in pairs or groups. Over thirty different substances may be involved in drug-assisted rapes, the most common one being alcohol. The drugs take effect quickly, causing drowsiness, vomiting or unconsciousness and the victim often has no memory of the attack.

There are a number of precautions that can be taken to avoid spiked drinks:

- **Don't accept drinks from strangers.**

- **Wherever possible watch drinks being poured.**

- **Never leave drinks unattended, even if you go to the toilet.**

- **Buy bottled drinks and keep your thumb over the top of the bottle.**

- **If your drink looks, smells or tastes unusual, don't take another sip.**

- **Keep an eye on your friends and their drinks too.**

- **Signs of having your drink spiked include nausea and vomiting, or sudden drunkenness that's far too strong for the amount of alcohol you've had to drink.**

- **If you or your friends start to feel unexpectedly sick or drowsy, take action immediately – you may not have long. Tell a trusted friend the drink may have been spiked, and if you're in a pub or club tell the security staff too.**

- **If you suspect your friend has had a drink spiked, call an ambulance and don't leave them alone.**

DRINK PROBLEMS

Someone who is developing alcohol dependency may fall into one or more of these patterns:

- **Tolerance: needing to drink more and more to get the same effect**

- **Alcohol becoming their priority over friends, partners, work, study and other interests**

- **Becoming stressed, upset or angry if they can't get a drink**

- **Physical withdrawal symptoms such as shakiness or sickness**

- **Drinking to avoid withdrawal symptoms, possibly drinking in the morning**

- **Hiding the amount they drink or lying about it**

About 15 per cent of young people show some signs of alcohol dependency, with males four times more likely to be affected than females. If you are being affected by your own or someone else's problem drinking, it can be a great help to have some skilled counselling. Try talking to Drinkline on 0345 320202.

DRUGS

Around 50 per cent of young people admit to having tried at least one recreational drug, most commonly cannabis. Drug culture permeates through large sections of society in this country, including the student population. Many students never take drugs, some dabble for a short period and then stop, and others go on to become regular users.

There's no point in me getting all preachy and saying that all drug users get ill, die, go mad, become a junkie or get arrested and thrown in prison. However, there are genuine risks related to drug use and bad things can happen to anyone because the effects are unpredictable. Drugs are not compulsory and if you don't want to take them then a polite but firm 'no thanks' should do the trick.

Various people talk a lot of rubbish about drugs and it can be hard to know what information to trust. Read around the subject with a critical eye, understand how the law works and get an idea of the physical and mental effects. Whether you choose to take drugs or not, be aware of the problems that can arise, and how to help someone who is in trouble.

Certain factors increase the risks of drugs. For example:

- **History of mental illness**
- **Physical health problems**
- **Unfamiliar surroundings**
- **Going off alone to use drugs**
- **Buying drugs from strangers**
- **Using needles, especially shared ones**
- **Mixing different drugs**
- **Taking large amounts of drugs in one go**

Mixing drugs increases the chance of something going wrong. Some drugs are stronger when they're added to other ones, and certain combinations mask the symptoms of an overdose. Prescription drugs can lead to fatalities if they're mixed with certain recreational drugs.

DRUG FIRST AID
If someone is unwell try to find the first-aid person if you're in a club and if in doubt call an ambulance. Someone who is showing signs of panic and anxiety should be led away from crowded areas, loud noises and bright lights. Talk to them in a gentle voice and reassure them that it's going to be OK. Get them to breathe slowly. If you can't get through to them at all, send someone off to get help.

Overheating can happen as a combination of hot clubs, drugs and dehydration. The signs include dizziness, tiredness, cramps in arms and legs, dark urine and difficulty peeing. Sit someone who looks overheated down in a cooler, quiet place and get them to sip a pint of water very slowly.

Splash a little tepid water on their face or neck or wipe them down with a damp towel.

Someone who collapses should be treated as an emergency. Try to rouse them gently but don't shake them hard. If they don't come round, call out for help and loosen any tight clothing they're wearing. Check to see if they are breathing. If they are breathing put them into the recovery position on their left side with their right arm and leg bent, making sure their head is back and their airway is open. If they are not breathing, they need mouth-to-mouth resuscitation. If you don't know how to do this, put them into the recovery position and wait for the first-aider to arrive.

DRUGS AND THE LAW

Most people think that the term 'supply' means dealing or selling drugs in large amounts. It also includes selling tiny amounts of drugs to friends or giving them away for free. Having drugs on you or at home is classed as possession, and that includes storing or carrying them for someone else. If you are found with a large amount of drugs on you, this carries more serious penalties. Driving under the influence applies to drug-driving as much as drink-driving and you can be charged under the Road Traffic Act 1988.

Things you should know:

- **Allowing people to take drugs in your house can get you a conviction, even if you don't take any drugs yourself.**

- **Your uni may take a strong anti-drugs stance and throw you off your course if you get caught with drugs.**

- **A major drug conviction can mess up your employment prospects and freedom to travel.**

Classes and penalties

Some substances are covered by the Misuse of Drugs Act 1971 while others are regulated by the Medicines Act. Class A drugs include Ecstasy, heroin, cocaine, crack and LSD, and the maximum penalty for possession is seven years in prison and an unlimited fine. Maximum penalty for supply is a life sentence and an unlimited fine. Class B drugs include amphetamines. The maximum penalty for their possession is five years in prison and a fine, and supply can bring up to fourteen years in prison and a fine. Class Cs include mild tranquillisers, cannabis and anabolic steroids. Possession of drugs such as temazepam can get someone up to two years in prison and a fine, but for most Class Cs possession may be permitted if it's for personal use. These are of course the maximum penalties and they don't tend to be applied to first-time offenders or people caught with tiny amounts of drugs.

THE DRUGS

CANNABIS

What is it?: Leaves or tips of the *Cannabis sativa* plant, containing active ingredient THC.

Alias: Marijuana, weed, hash, grass, dope, draw and many more.

How is it used?: Smoked as a joint, smoked in pipe or eaten.

Effects: Users feel relaxed, happy and quiet, or giggly or talkative. Someone who has been smoking heavily may have red eyes, a dry mouth and an attack of the munchies.

Risks: Paranoia, anxiety, nausea. Heavy use may affect short-term memory.

AMPHETAMINES

What are they?: Group of synthetic stimulants, up to 95 per cent impure. Sold as an off-white, greyish or pinkish powder that may contain small crystals, or small pills.

Alias: Speed, whizz, uppers.

How is it used?: Snorted, rubbed onto gums or swallowed. Some forms may be smoked or injected.

Effects: Users feel energetic, wide awake and chatty. After use there may be a comedown with feelings of depression.

Risks: Irritability, aggression, paranoia and psychosis. Overdose. Addiction. Injecting makes overdose more likely, plus risk of HIV and hepatitis infection.

NITRITES (POPPERS)

What are they?: Alkyl nitrites – liquids sold in small bottles.

Alias: Poppers, amyl or brand names such as TNT.

How are they used?: Vapours are inhaled.

Effects: Cause a head rush lasting two minutes or so, often followed by headache. Dizziness, light-headedness or weakness.

Risks: Poisonous if swallowed, skin burns, collapse, flammable. Unsafe for anyone with heart or blood pressure conditions. Users may forget about safer sex.

Legal: Possession legal, but not supply.

LSD

What is it?: Lysergic acid diethylamide, a hallucinogen. Sold dotted onto paper squares, or in tiny tablets or capsules.

Alias: acid, trips, tabs.

How is it used?: Blotting papers are licked, tablets swallowed.

Effects: Takes around twenty minutes to an hour for effects to be felt, can go on for twelve to twenty hours. The experience, or trip, varies – can include sensations of time slowing down or speeding up, and distortions of colours, sounds and shapes. They can be funny or enjoyable (good trips), or highly unpleasant (bad trips).

Risks: Panic or paranoia. Users can injure themselves accidentally or deliberately. Flashbacks, where part of the trip is relived, can happen weeks or months after taking acid.

MAGIC MUSHROOMS

What are they?: Most commonly *Psilocybe semilanceata* mushrooms, which grow naturally in Britain. Picked fresh or sold dried.

Alias: 'shrooms, mushies, majicks.

How are they used?: Eaten raw, cooked or made into tea.

Effects: After about thirty minutes a trip begins, lasting up to nine hours. Users may feel giggly and happy, and sounds, colours, shapes and time may feel distorted.

Risks: Picking the wrong type of mushroom and being poisoned. Bad trips, diarrhoea, flashbacks.

Legal: Possessing raw mushrooms is not illegal. If they are prepared for use they are Class A.

ECSTASY

What is it?: Pure Ecstasy is MDMA (3,4-methylenedioxymethamphetamine), a stimulant with very mild hallucinogenic effects, mainly sold in pill form. Newer pills contain less MDMA and are more likely to contain other drugs.

Alias: E, pills, XTC or named after pictures on pills.

How is it used?: Usually swallowed, sometimes snorted or smoked.

Effects: Take thirty minutes or so to take effect. Users feel energetic, euphoric and more in tune with their surroundings, music and other people. Body temperature can increase and jaw muscles tighten. Effects last three to six hours with a gradual comedown.

Risks: Anxiety, panic attacks, paranoia, epileptic fits. Dehydration, overheating and collapse, death. Long-term effects uncertain, but may include memory loss and depression.

SOLVENTS (AEROSOLS, GASES AND GLUES)

What are they?: Volatile chemicals found in some paints, aerosol cans, lighter fuel, glue, cleaning fluids and many more.

Alias: Glue, gas.

How are they used?: Sniffed from liquids on rags or inhaled directly.

Effects: Similar to drunkenness but lasts for a shorter period. Sometimes hallucinations.

Risks: Headache, rashes, vomiting, blackouts, death from choking and irregular heartbeat. On average six people die from solvent abuse every week in the UK.

Legal: Not illegal to possess.

COCAINE
What is it?: Stimulant made from leaves of the coca shrub. Sold in wraps of whitish powder.

Alias: Coke, charlie, powder, gack.

How is it used?: Chopped into lines on flat surface and snorted. Sometimes injected.

Effects: Users feel wide awake and extra confident. Raises body temperature and heartbeats. Effects last around thirty minutes.

Risks: Psychological dependency, damage to nose, heart attacks, overdose. Anxiety, depression and sexual dysfunction. Overdose more likely when injected.

CRACK
What is it?: Smokable form of cocaine. Sold in small lumps.

Alias: Base, wash, stones, rock.

How is it used?: Smoked in pipe, glass tube or on tinfoil.

Effects: Similar to cocaine but more intense and short-lived.

Risks: Cravings, addiction, overdose.

TRANQUILLISERS

What are they?: Group of prescription drugs with sedating effects. Includes tablets and capsules such as Valium, Mogadon, Rohypnol and temazepam.

Alias: Downers, benzos, jellies.

How are they used?: Mostly swallowed, sometimes injected.

Effects: Users may feel calm, sleepy or relaxed.

Risks: Psychological and physical addiction. Overdose when mixed with alcohol, memory loss. Injecting may lead to gangrene.

Legal: Class C. Possession an arrestable offence if user does not have valid prescription.

HEROIN

What is it?: Drug made from morphine, extracted from opium poppies. Medical grade opiates tend to be white powder, street heroin is brownish in colour.

Alias: Brown, smack, H, horse, skag, gear.

How is it used?: Smoked, snorted, or injected.

Effects: Feelings of comfort, relaxation or sleepiness. Sickness and vomiting.

Risks: Constipation, overdose, coma, physical dependency. Infections and abscesses from injecting and sharing needles.

DEPENDENCY

When a user becomes drug-dependent, they have a strong desire for the drug, often needing to take increasing amounts to get the same effect. When dependency develops, it can cause serious problems with relationships, work and money. Many users give up on their own, but others prefer to have the support of their doctor or a specialist organisation.

DRUG AND LEGAL ADVICE

TALK TO FRANK

General information and advice about all street drugs

Helpline: 0800 77 66 00, open 24 hours every day.

DRUGSCOPE

Information sheets and independent up-to-date research about all drugs.

Website: www.drugscope.org.uk, telephone: 020 7928 1211.

CHAPTER 5: HOUSING

Home sweet home.

The main types of student accommodation include:

- **Halls of residence**
- **University houses and flats**
- **Privately rented shared houses and flats**
- **Student-owned places**

HALLS

Most halls are near campus, and charge fees at the beginning of every term.

Pros	Cons
Very sociable	If it's catered you may hate the food
Rent may include food and bills, easier to budget	Can be noisy when you're trying to sleep or revise
Facilities such as common rooms, laundrette, cleaners	Many rules and regulations
More safety features than most private housing	Small basic rooms can have a 'rabbit hutch' feel
Close to campus	

WHAT UNIVERSITY HALLS ARE REALLY LIKE

Hall facilities, layouts and décor are variable. In recent years there's been a move towards self-catering. There are still some enormous buildings that house hundreds of students, with several rooms on each open corridor, plus shared bathrooms and toilets. They tend to have a staffed security entrance and include lighting and heating in with their fees. It's more common to find bigger buildings split into blocks of self-contained flats or several low-rise blocks of flats arranged around a communal area. There's usually a laundrette and payphones, but larger halls come into their own with telly or games rooms, or bars.

RULES, REGULATIONS, DISPUTES

Some halls are stricter than others. If your hall has a single security entrance, there tend to be rules about who you can or can't let in, having parties or overnight guests. You're normally expected to sign people in and out, and give warning of who is staying with you. Problems with neighbours or flatmates can be sorted out amongst yourselves or through mediation with hall wardens or the students' union. If you're asked to move out because of something you've done, you need specialist advice from your student advice centre or a specialist organisation such as Shelter.

PRIVATE HALLS

These are halls of residence that are built and run by private companies, let to students under regulations imposed by the university. The main contractors are Jarvis, Unite, Opal and Servite.

RENTING PRIVATELY

Pros	Cons
Rent is cheaper than most hall fees	Can be further away from campus
More privacy, fewer noisy people around	Some student landlords are dodgy
Freedom	Bills can pile up
	Quiet during holidays

WHAT SHARING IS REALLY LIKE
Most students rent shared houses with friends. These places are usually in the cheaper parts of town and can be very basic.

WHO TO LIVE WITH
You're going to be seeing people at their worst: bleary eyed at breakfast, hungover or ill, heartbroken after relationships end or at breaking point before exams. Easy-going, fairly considerate people you have something in common with are the safest bet.

FINDING A PLACE
Start looking in early spring if you can to get the pick of the best places. Be prepared to look around for a while to find somewhere suitable. Get an idea of rents from older students or the students' union, and ask where the best areas in town are.

Try the university accommodation service or notice boards, the local paper or internet accommodation sites. You can also try accommodation agencies, but look for ones with good reputations and never pay any money upfront.

If you see something promising, follow it up quickly. Check locations and arrange viewings. Get as many of your group as you can together to view properties that sound good. Follow these safety tips:

- **Never go there alone, always go with someone else.**

- **Go during daylight hours.**

- **Tell someone exactly where you're going and when you'll be back.**

- **If you get a bad feeling, trust your instincts and leave.**

Things to ask:

- **What bills are tenants liable for? Average costs?**

- **Is rent cheaper during holidays?**

- How much is the monthly rent and deposit?
- What type of heating and hot water supply?
- Can you talk to current tenants?

Important things to look for:

- Distance from shops and public transport.
- Parking spaces or bike storage.
- The feel of the local area. Safe at night? Pleasant neighbours?
- Look at everything (each room, inside cupboards, roof tiles, back of house).
- The size of every bedroom. Is there a boxroom nobody wants?
- Strong front and back doors and gates with decent locks, secure windows.
- Signs of damp or mildew, such as a musty smell or black spores.
- Draughty doors, cracked windows.
- Infestations: mouse droppings, slime trails, dead insects.
- Safety certificates for all gas appliances, carbon monoxide detectors.
- State of electrical wiring and appliances.
- Easy exit in case of fire. Smoke alarms, fire extinguishers.
- State of repair of the kitchen and bathroom.
- What's included: crockery, pans and cutlery, freezer, washing machine?
- General state of furniture, mattresses, carpets, etc.
- Telephone landline and sockets.

SIGNING UP FOR A PLACE

Once you've found a place, you need to sign a contract and pay deposits. The contract is legally binding so read the small print before signing. If anything seems unreasonable or confusing, get it checked by the university accommodation office or your local Citizens Advice Bureau. Your contract will probably be an 'assured shorthold tenancy', lasting for at least six months. Check whether it's a single or joint tenancy agreement. With single tenancy each person is only liable for their share of rent and bills, but joint tenancy means that if one of you defaults on the rent, the rest of you can be charged.

Check the following:

- **Start and end dates of contract**

- **Monthly rent and deposit**

- **Charges for late rent**

- **Landlord's responsibilities**

- **Landlord's full contact details**

- **Notice period**

Once you've all signed the contract, you should be given your own copy before you move in. Keep it safe, in case you need to refer to it later. An oral contract is also legally binding, but hard to prove in court.

The inventory is a list of everything in the property, and when you are given one check thoroughly around the house to see if it's correct. If you aren't shown an inventory, ask for one.

The deposit is a sum of money, usually the same as a month's rent, you pay to the landlord as security. The landlord can keep all or part of this money to cover repairs and cleaning. You should be given a receipt.

WHEN YOU MOVE IN. . .

Allocate rooms as fairly as you can. Flip coins, draw straws or pull names out of a hat if you can't decide who's going to get which room. If there's one tiny bedroom and the rest of the rooms are a decent size, perhaps the occupant could pay less rent. Locate water and gas stopcocks and electrical fuse box, in case of emergencies. Find electricity and gas meters and take your own readings. Decide on home entertainment.

COMMON FLASHPOINTS

Most of the time housemates rub along together fine. But there are a few things that cause rows:

- **Dirt and mess**
  Keep your own mess to yourself, and clean up as you go with dropped food and spills. Get your washing-up done. Spread nasty tasks around equally using a rota for emptying the bin, cleaning the loo, vacuuming and mopping floors.

- **Hogging**
  Get everyone to agree to time limits for using the shower in the morning or the phone in the evening. If there's only one TV, you have to be prepared to negotiate for the programmes you want to watch.

- **Noise**
  Sleep deprivation can drive anyone crazy. Avoid clattering around if you're the first one up in the morning; try not to talk loudly if you come home late and pissed up. Use headphones late at night.

- **Decorating**
  Don't make big design statements in communal areas without agreeing it with everyone else first.

- **Lovers and mates**
  Avoid overkill by agreeing partners and pals only come over on certain nights of the week, up to a maximum of maybe three nights. Having old friends to stay can be cool for you, but may cause resentment with everyone else. Check with flatmates first that it's OK.

- **Money**
  There's always one person who's late with the rent, forgets to pay
  their share of the bills and doesn't see why they should chip in a few
  quid for the kitty. Don't let the situation drag on for too long. You can't
  afford to carry someone indefinitely, even if he or she is a mate.

THE BILLS, BILLS, BILLS

Make sure bills don't all end up in one person's name – share them out if
you can or get all the names on each bill. When another scary bill plops
onto the doormat, try to pay it reasonably promptly or you could be in for
red bills, disconnections and more.

If you're struggling to pay, contact the supplier as soon as possible to let
them know you are experiencing difficulty. If a flatmate has done a runner
and left bills unpaid, contact the landlord and the supplier quickly. The
landlord could give you money out of their deposit to cover the shortfall or
the company may let you off part of the bill.

- **Electricity and gas**
  Shop around for the best deal, and don't sign up with salespeople who
  come door-to-door offering you price cuts.

- **Water**
  Find out if you're responsible for paying water rates. If you are, check
  you're not paying too much. Some areas have metered water, so watch
  out for high charges and learn how to conserve water.

- **Council tax**
  If it's a house full of students, you're not liable to pay any council tax
  on the property. You just need to send the council an exemption
  certificate from the university.

- **Telephone**
  This is the biggest culprit for money arguments. Some houses keep a
  logbook by the phone to say what numbers they called and when, so
  it's clear who made expensive calls. Get an itemised bill, and do the

sums. It's an equal share of the standing charge, line rental and discounts, plus the individual person's call charges, then the whole number is multiplied by 1.175 (to add on their VAT at 17.5%), to give the person's final share of the bill.

- **Internet**
  If you're studying with a computer at home, get internet access. See if you're in a broadband area.

- **Rentals**
  Renting a washing machine is cheaper than going to the laundrette. You may also like a big communal TV for the living room.

- **TV licence**
  If you don't get one you could be looking at a £1000 fine. The licence people have a pretty good idea of where the student houses are in town, so your chances of getting caught are high. Telephone 0870 241 6468 for payments and rebates or use the website: www.tv-l.co.uk.

- **Communal items**
  It's easier to put money for toilet rolls, bin bags, cleaning products and shared food like milk or margarine in a kitty. Or take turns buying them.

TROUBLESHOOTING

Security advice is covered in Chapter 9, but read on for the rest of the problem-busters.

Landlords are obliged to keep the following in proper working order: exterior structure of the house, water, gas, electricity, sewerage, space heating and hot water. If there's anything wrong with your property, notify the landlord in writing as well as telephoning. Allow 48 hours for emergency works and 1 or 2 weeks for other works. If the landlord doesn't sort things out, go to your accommodation service for more advice, or speak to a Citizens Advice Bureau or housing charity Shelter (see Contacts).

BRRR, CHILLY BREEZES
Make sure the landlord fixes the boiler, central heating, broken windows or damaged window frames. You can buy cheap clear plastic seals in big DIY stores to cover whole windows and keep the heat in.

To save money, most students don't heat their houses much. If it's very cold outside or snowing, put the heating on at least once every day or pipes can freeze.

EVERYTHING'S GONE GREEN AND FURRY
If it's simple condensation, make sure your airbricks aren't blocked, and open the windows when needed to let out steam. Wipe mouldy areas down with an anti-mildew product.

WHAT'S THAT SCUTTLING NOISE?
Let the landlord know straight away if there's any kind of infestation, and keep food firmly shut away in cupboards, jars and nibble-proof boxes. If your landlord is unhelpful, try the environmental health office at your local council.

FIRE SAFETY – SAVE YOUR OWN LIFE
If your house doesn't have smoke detectors, get some as soon as you can because smoke and fumes can kill quickly and silently. They only cost a few pounds and they're worth every penny.

Common causes of fires in student houses:

- **Candles: never leave them unattended.**
- **Cigarettes and joints: don't smoke in bed.**
- **Kitchen fires: avoid using chip pans if you can. Put pan fires out by covering them with a damp wrung-out tea towel and turning the cooker off if possible. Leave the pan where it is, damp towel in place, until it has cooled.**

79

- **Heaters: don't cover them or knock them over while they're on, and don't hang clothes on them to dry unless they're standard radiators (no bar or flame).**

- **Electrical: report loose sockets and don't overload with plugs and extensions.**

Keep fire exits free from rubbish or bicycles. Keep keys near to doors and windows to allow a speedy exit, but not in view of passing burglars. Go around the house checking ashtrays and closing doors before you go to bed at night.

If you discover a fire:

- **Raise the alarm by shouting loudly.**

- **Get everyone out of the house without putting yourself at risk.**

- **Shut doors behind you and call 999.**

- **If you're trapped upstairs, shut doors and stay low to avoid smoke, and throw bedding onto the ground to soften your landing. Lower yourself out of the window.**

- **If you can't jump, keep your head out of the window to breathe fresh air, continue calling for help.**

- **If clothes catch fire, roll on the floor to put flames out.**

Find out more about fire safety at www.firekills.gov.uk.

GAS AND CARBON MONOXIDE
Carbon monoxide is a silent killer, responsible for around thirty unnecessary deaths every year. It can seep out of old or unserviced gas appliances, and be made worse by blocked chimneys and flues. Landlords are legally obliged to have every gas appliance checked yearly by a CORGI-registered engineer and should show you the safety certificate within one month. To check on any engineer, call CORGI on 01256 372300. Never block

the ventilation that the appliances need, such as flues and airbricks. Although there may be no danger signs, make sure your appliances do not show any of the following: staining or discolouration, burning with a lazy orange or yellow flame or a strange smell when in use. To be on the safe side, get a carbon monoxide detector.

Carbon monoxide poisoning is hard to spot and the symptoms can mimic flu, food poisoning or depression. Be on the lookout for headaches, dizziness, muscle weakness, tiredness, vomiting or nausea, diarrhoea, stomach pain or chest pain. It can come on slowly or be sudden. If you think there's a chance you have carbon monoxide poisoning, speak to your GP or go to Accident and Emergency at your local hospital.

Gas leaks are rare, but if you smell gas in your home:

- **Immediately put out cigarettes.**

- **Open doors and windows.**

- **Turn off gas supply.**

- **Don't switch anything electrical off or on, not even a light switch.**

- **Get everyone out of the house and call Transco free on 0800 111 999. You will get a free visit from an engineer.**

For more information look at www.corgi-gas-safety.com.

WATER AND PLUMBING
Dripping taps and leaky baths or shower trays are the landlord's responsibility. If there are large leaks, turn off the water using the stopcock, put buckets under drips and ask for it to be fixed urgently. Blocked sinks are your responsibility if you've let hair or grease build up.

MEET THE NEIGHBOURS
Try to get on with your neighbours and make a general effort not to piss them off with loud noise and late-night parties. If you're having problems

with your neighbours such as arguments about noise, or harassment, speak to someone at the student's union about it. They may have a mediation service available, or can help report incidents to police.

LANDLORDS, WONDERFUL AND WANKY

Some landlords are very professional. If you have a good landlord, recommend them to other people when you leave. When your landlord is dodgy, don't be abusive or withhold rent; go through proper legal channels.

HARASSMENT AND ILLEGAL EVICTION

Your landlord or (or their agent) is not allowed to:

- **Turn up unannounced and let themselves in, unless it's an emergency**

- **Tamper with locks, electricity, gas or water**

- **Interfere with possessions**

- **Threaten violence or use force**

- **Evict you without going through the correct legal process**

- **Show sexual or racial discrimination**

If any of these happen, seek immediate help from the students' union and your council's tenancy relations officer.

GETTING YOUR DEPOSIT BACK

Students are particularly vulnerable to unscrupulous practices concerning deposits, and need to be careful when leaving premises at the end of their tenancy.

- **When you move out, clean thoroughly, and check everything on the inventory is present and in good working order.**

- 'Clean' means sparkling clean. Wipe walls, wash stained carpets, wash net curtains and scrub floors. Clean the hob and inside the oven thoroughly. Make sure there's no rubbish outside the house.

- Pay all bills and show proof of payment to the landlord.

- Ask the landlord to come round and inspect.

- Get independent witnesses to check the place is in good condition on the day you move out. Take photographs.

- Give back all keys and get a receipt.

- Agree a timeframe for return of deposit.

Should your deposit fail to turn up, write to your landlord, and contact your nearest advice centre. Students who suspect the deposit may be wrongly withheld sometimes withhold their last month's rent. It puts you on dodgy legal ground as you're breaking the terms of your contract, but you may decide it's the best way. In which case follow the moving out checklist above carefully and keep evidence. If your deposit is being held unfairly, the only chance to get it back is by taking the landlord to your local small claims court.

CHAPTER 6: MONEY

It's never been more important for students to get to grips with money.

This chapter covers:

- **Student banking and the best accounts**
- **Student loans, access funds and bursaries**
- **Expenses and budgeting**
- **Money saving tips to keep bills down**
- **Coping with debt stress and controlling borrowing**

STUDENT BANKING

Student accounts are similar to most current accounts, but tend to have extras like interest-free overdrafts.

WHICH ACCOUNT IS RIGHT FOR ME?

When choosing an account, consider:

- **The amount of interest free overdraft – how much they'll let you have in the first year and final year.**
- **Arranged overdraft rates and fees.**
- **Unarranged overdraft costs.**
- **Where their cash machines (ATMs) are, or whether you can use their card free in other ATMs.**
- **Where their nearest branch is.**

- **Ease of paying in cheques and cash.**

- **Interest paid on a positive balance (savings).**

- **Arrangements for graduates.**

Once you've opened your account, compare banks every year or so. If your account is not competitive, switch.

For student banking offers and general money advice, see www.studentmoney.org.

CREDIT CARDS
Cards are the most expensive way to borrow. Students who use them as overdraft extensions can carry crippling debt for years. They're useful when travelling, but read the small print.

KEEPING THE BANK MANAGER SWEET
If you're about to go over the edge of your agreed overdraft limit, phone the bank quickly to avoid being slapped with fees for stroppy letters or interest charges.

INCOMING MONEY

The main sources of money are student loans, help from parents and wages from part-time jobs. Students may also qualify for additional bursaries, grants and benefits.

STUDENT LOANS
Student loans help cover living costs and tuition fees. They are the cheapest way to borrow.

APPLYING
After you've applied for your university course, your local award authority handles the first stage of your loan application. Interest on the loan is linked

to the rate of inflation, so in real terms the total amount that borrowers repay is equivalent to the amount they have borrowed. Part of all student support loans are means-tested, and you can choose whether you wish to apply for this. There's more information available from the Department for Education and Skills (DfES) (see Contacts).

When your award authority sends you your support notification or eligibility notice, complete the loan request form and return to the Student Loans Company (see Contacts section). From this point onwards, the Student Loans Company (SLC) becomes responsible for the administration of your loan. The SLC sends you a loan acknowledgement letter, followed by a payment schedule letter approximately fourteen days before the start of term.

PICKING UP THE MONEY

If the SLC have received authorisation in enough time, you receive your first 'BACS' electronic money transfer payment direct into your bank or building society account in time for the start of your course.

HARDSHIP LOANS

If you're in extreme financial difficulties, you may be eligible for an extra hardship loan. You need to have applied for a full student loan and have received the first instalment of it. Contact the student loans officer at your college or university, then your college can assess your circumstances.

REPAYING

As soon you graduate and start earning more than £15,000 per year, repayments (9 per cent of anything earned over £15,000) begin, unless you apply to defer your payments for 12 months. The money is normally collected by the Inland Revenue via the employer.

PARENTS

If your have all or part of the funds available, sit down together and work out how much money you'll need for your living expenses. Set a realistic budget, and try not to go back begging for handouts.

If you're estranged from your parents, make this very clear when you're being means-tested by your local education authority. You may get special consideration when applying for loans.

JOBS
Choose your type of employment carefully, and try not to work too many hours each week, otherwise coursework suffers badly. Don't pay too much tax on your earnings – fill in the right forms when you start work (see Chapter 7).

ACCESS FUNDS AND OTHER FUNDS
Your university can provide access/hardship funds; ask for the application forms at the union building. Should you qualify, you'll get a non-repayable sum. Students' unions may also make small emergency loans.

GRANTS & BURSARIES FROM CHARITIES AND TRUSTS
Charities and trusts all over the UK give money to students. Ask at your local library, church or town hall.

In the careers library, check out *The Directory of Grant Making Trusts* by the Charities Aid Foundation or *The Educational Grants Directory* by Alan French, Dave Griffiths, Tom Traynor and Sarah Wiggins, published by Directory of Social Change.

Your university department should have information about scholarships, bursaries and other funding or gifts-in kind from various educational foundations.

GOVERNMENT GRANTS
Students from poorer backgrounds may qualify for government means-tested grants. These don't have to be repaid.

SPONSORSHIP
Certain degrees attract sponsorship from industrial companies, the army and so on, with extra money for living expenses, and the opportunity to do

paid work during vacations. After graduation, sponsored students are often expected to work for their backers for a few years.

EXTRA EDUCATIONAL LOANS

Many banks and building societies offer educational loans, some of which run in conjunction with government schemes.

OUTGOING MONEY

Once you've sorted out a student bank account and maximised your income, you need to control your cash flow. If you mess up your budget don't give up completely, start again.

TUITION FEES

Some students will have to pay university tuition fees. This is means-tested on a sliding scale through your local educational award authority. Most universities let you pay in instalments.

LIVING EXPENSES

Think about:

- **Rent**

- **Insurance**

- **Main bills: electricity, gas, water, telephone, mobile phone**

- **Other bills: TV licence, laundry**

- **One offs: books, household items, deposits**

- **Groceries, toiletries**

- **Stationery**

- **Clothes**

- **Entertainment**

- **Transport**

- **Birthdays, Christmas**

- **Treats**

BUDGETING

Here are a few basic budgeting skills, plus a wide range of tricks and tips for saving money on all kinds of expenses.

BASIC BUDGETING SKILLS

Once you know your basic living costs, start making a budget. Work it out on a termly, monthly or weekly basis. Write your budgets down and try your hardest to stick to them. Keep track of everything you spend, and review regularly.

One way to cope with a tight budget is by working in cash for weekly spending. Put the cash card away somewhere safe. This leaves money for groceries, toiletries, the laundrette, travel, going out, photocopying and so on. Once it's gone, don't go back to the bank for more.

For more help with your budgeting skills, try reading *Money for Life* by Alvin Hall (Coronet, £5.99), or www.fool.co.uk and www.moneysavingexpert.com.

MONEY-SAVING TIPS

General tips:

- **Claim all benefits for prescription charges, dental care and so on.**

- **Tell the local council you're exempt from paying council tax.**

Utilities bills:

- **Shop around for gas, electricity, telephone and internet connection deals. Try online price comparison services.**

- If you are sent an estimate for a bill, read the meter yourself.
- Don't leave TVs on standby.
- Switch your thermostat down half a degree.
- Don't boil a kettle full of water for one cuppa.
- Stick to 'off peak' call times whenever possible.

Mobile phone bills:

- Although the cost per unit is higher, a pay-as-you-go mobile is the easiest way to keep your total bill manageable.
- If you're disciplined, a good line rental deal may be cheaper. Shop around.
- If your mate is a chatterbox, send them a text message instead.
- Use free university email and messenger software.

Food bills:

- Buy in bulk with friends.
- Go to fruit and veg markets just before they close.
- Buy from bargain supermarkets (Aldi, Lidl or Netto) or stick to bargain ranges.
- Make meals at home based on cheap filling foods like pasta, rice, potatoes, beans or bread.
- Buy seasonal local fruit, vegetables, fish or meat.
- Plan weekly recipes and food shopping; write a shopping list.

Clothes and toiletries:

- Go for BOGOFs (buy one get one free).

- Use cheap make-up ranges such as **Rimmel** or **Maybelline**.

- Buy designer labels in sales or second-hand, and mix them with high-street and junk-shop finds. Or buy high-street versions from **Topshop**, **H&M**, etc.

- For an individual look, customise second-hand clothes or make your own.

- Cheap accessories such as belts or jewellery bring old outfits up to date.

Other bills:

- Some bills are cheaper if you pay by direct debit.

- Cut transport costs by cycling or using student discount cards.

DEBT

Student debt is a fact of life. If you live on a reasonable budget, your debts should remain manageable.

MANAGING YOUR DEBTS
Don't fall into the common trap of thinking 'Well, I'm ten grand in debt now, so I might as well be twenty grand in debt.'

ARE YOU IN SERIOUS DEBT?
There are several signs that suggest you're building up an unmanageable debt:

- You're too scared to work out how much you owe in total.

- You avoid opening your bank statements and bills, throw them away or hide them.

- You can barely cover each minimum monthly credit card repayment.

- You let unauthorised overdrafts build up, because you can't talk to the bank.

- You're taking out loans or other credit to pay off other debts.

- You get angry letters from creditors or visits from bailiffs.

- You owe so much money to your university for rent or tuition fees they've threatened to withhold awarding you your degree.

HOW TO SORT BAD DEBTS OUT

If your debts are out of control, the first thing to do is admit there's a serious problem. Work out exactly how much you do owe and to whom. List everything: overdraft, student loans, other unsecured loans, credit cards, money owed to mates and family, hire-purchase agreements and so on. Then prioritise these debts while you get a handle on your spending. Your main aim is to keep a roof over your head and to avoid getting your utilities cut off – make sure your rent and bills are covered first. Make a strict budget for your everyday outgoings, and stick to it, even if that means unpleasant cutbacks.

Target anything that's being charged at higher rates of interest, such as credit cards, and sort that out as a priority. Wherever possible, switch the balance onto cards with lower APRs so you're paying as little interest as possible. Then tackle remaining debts with high-interest charges. Make a debt repayment plan, including what you're able to pay everyone each month.

If you've missed payments, write to the companies involved and explain your financial situation. Offer to make reduced payments and pay the debt off over a longer period of time. Most companies will agree (it costs so much to take legal action against you or send in bailiffs). If anyone is threatening you with court proceedings, or has already started them, you urgently need advice from an organisation such as a Citizens Advice Bureau, or Student Debtline (see Contacts). Harassment from your creditors, such as making nuisance visits and phone calls, or using threatening and abusive language is illegal.

Although it's tempting, avoid commercial companies that offer to consolidate debts. There are several free advice services that can help you to manage your debts much more effectively, so use them instead.

Some people choose to be declared bankrupt to avoid their creditors, but think very carefully about this option. Assets may still be taken to pay off your debts, you'll have to close your bank or building society account, and it can damage your credit rating for years. Student Loans Company debts are not wiped out by bankruptcy.

COPING WITH DEBT STRESS

Large, out-of-control debts are highly stressful. If you take steps to make your debts more manageable, you should find the emotional strain lessens. Try not to keep it bottled up; talk to a mate, a partner or family members, or you may prefer to speak to someone confidentially. In that case, try your student union, the university counselling service or a non-profit debt service for specialist support and advice.

CHAPTER 7: WORK AND CAREERS

Whether it's just a bit of spare cash to pay for your social life, or the start of your brilliant career, you need to have a good idea of what you want and how to get it.

This chapter includes information on:

- **Part-time jobs**
- **Holiday work at home and abroad**
- **Work experience, placements and projects**
- **Tax and workers' rights**
- **Job-hunting and career choices**

PART-TIME JOBS

Over 40 per cent of students take on part-time jobs during term time, working for an average of 13 hours per week. An increasing number of students say they work just to survive. The National Union of Students recommends that you take on no more than ten hours of paid work per week.

If you're going to get a part-time job, think about the hours you'd like to work, how far you're willing to travel and the types of work you're prepared to do.

Pros	Cons
Source of extra money	Can interfere with study
Good for CV	May be poorly paid
Make new friends and contacts	Can be menial and boring
Develops transferable skills	

WHERE TO FIND WORK

Start looking for jobs around the university. There may be term-time work available on campus in the bars and shops. Local employers place ads on jobs notice boards in the student union, with the careers service or the job shop. If your university has a job shop, visit for specialist advice about the local employment market. The National Association of Student Employment Services (NASES) covers all student job shops in the UK – see www.nases.org.uk.

Also try:

- **Commercial websites**
- **Job centre**
- **Local papers**
- **Recruitment agencies**
- **Dropping in on shops etc.**

WHAT TO EXPECT

Part-time work for students tends to be in retail, bars, clerical or office work, catering, and call centres.

- **Retail jobs are relatively easy to find, and they often need extra staff at weekends or during the evenings.**
- **Bar work can start quickly once you've got the job and there's the possibility of tips and socialising after the shifts. Usually finish late – insist on a free taxi.**
- **Office jobs can be anything from reception work to filing, but can pay OK and don't get your hands too dirty.**
- **Catering covers everything from fast food to cafés, staff canteens to high-class restaurants. You may go home exhausted and reeking of chip fat, and tips are variable.**

- **Call centres can be high-pressure environments and you need an excellent phone manner for telesales or customer care lines.**

GETTING PAID

Students pay income tax and national insurance. Tax is usually deducted from your earnings by your employer. Fill in a P46 form if you're working part-time during term to make sure you don't end up paying too much tax.

Most students don't earn enough to pay National Insurance (NI) contributions, but you still need an NI number to work in the UK. See www.inlandrevenue.gov.uk. International students need to fill in form P85.

Students who have children may be eligible for Working Families Tax Credit, and there are benefits for disabled students too. See www.direct.gov.uk.

Everyone should make sure that they're getting at least the national minimum wage. See www.hmrc.gov.uk/nmw/.

YOUR RIGHTS

Part-time workers are often confused about their rights. For example, if you're working longer than six hours at a time, you're entitled to a break of at least twenty minutes. The relationship between you and your employer is determined by your employment contract, so read it carefully. Spoken contracts are legally binding too. Employers are responsible for providing adequate insurance cover and training you in health and safety issues.

You also have statutory rights: all workers must be treated fairly and you should not be discriminated against because of your sex, race, disability or trade union membership. There's an excellent website called www.troubleatwork.org.uk.

HOLIDAY WORK

Stay in Britain, or combine work and travel to go just about anywhere in the world. Students who stay in this country often end up doing:

- **Clerical work**
- **Factory work**
- **Catering work**
- **Shop work**
- **Call-centre cover**
- **Tourism and leisure work**
- **Outdoor work: labouring, decorating, agricultural**

If you're working in the UK during vacations, and don't expect to exceed your personal tax allowance, ask your employer for form P38(S). This allows them to pay your wages without deducting tax.

Holiday work will be advertised in your university job shop, local temp agencies, your nearest job centre and on websites.

Working holidays abroad have the added advantage of doing some travelling before or afterwards. Try:

- **Teaching English as a foreign language (more about this in Chapter 10)**
- **Fruit or vegetable harvesting**
- **Chalet work or ski instruction**
- **Archaeological or conservation work**
- **Crewing on cruise ships or yachts**
- **Working with kids on holiday camps**

BUNAC (www.bunac.org.uk) offer non-profit overseas work/travel programmes that mostly fit into a long summer abroad, including Summer Camp USA.

Try *Work Your Way Around the World* by Susan Griffith, Vacation Work Publications, £12.95.

22

WORK PLACEMENTS

Relevant work experience can give you a competitive edge over other graduates when you enter the job market.

WHY DO WORK EXPERIENCE?

- Improves employment prospects
- A chance to see if it's right for you
- Earn while you learn
- Contacts

Speak to staff in your department to find out what they recommend and whether they have contacts in particular industries. Use your careers service for magazines, fact sheets, lists of vacancies and details of work-experience fairs.

WHAT'S AVAILABLE?

- Part of your degree: sandwich courses, projects, professional practice
- Holiday and part-time employment
- Structured internships with large organisations
- Voluntary work
- Mentoring and tutoring
- Work shadowing
- Overseas placements and exchanges

A good placement is set up with the aim of benefiting the student. You should have training, objectives, supervision and opportunities to ask questions and give feedback. Supervisors should protect your working rights, teach you and provide assessment at the end of the programme, preferably using guidelines from your university.

Start looking for work experience early and avoid the final-year rush. The Higher Education Careers Services Unit (CSU) runs the National Centre for Work Experience (NCWE, www.work-experience.org), a good place to start.

VOLUNTEERING

Offers the chance to give something back to the local (or worldwide) community, meet new friends and make work contacts. Looks great on a CV. Volunteer through your local volunteer bureau or through your university's branch of the national network of Student Community Action Groups (SCA). There are 180 groups around the UK, and 25,000 students get involved every year.

You can also contact the National Centre for Volunteering at Regents Wharf, 8 All Saints Street, London N1 9RL, telephone: 020 7520 8900, fax: 020 7520 8910, website: www.volunteering.org.uk.

JOB-HUNTING TOOLS AND SKILLS

A CV, or curriculum vitae, is a summary of your skills and experience. Most recruiters are frantically busy – if a CV or application form is messy or full of spelling mistakes, it'll be in the bin in seconds.

WRITE THE KILLER CV

- **Do your CV on a computer and keep a backup.**

- **Think about the format. Most employers will take your CV in an electronic format. If you're sending a printout, use decent quality white paper and black ink.**

- **Lay the text out simply. Allow enough white space between the sections of text so the pages don't look too cramped.**

- **Keep to two pages in length.**

- **Write your name at the top, not 'curriculum vitae'.**

- Divide text into sections for contact details, education, work experience and references.

- Don't waffle.

- Use dynamic language such as 'designed', 'attended', 'devised', 'organised'.

- Say what you've learned from various experiences.

- Show your CV to tutors, friends or the careers service. Check thoroughly for typing errors and mistakes.

- Never put an outright lie on your CV.

- If you're posting a CV, include a good covering letter and use an A4 envelope so they arrive unfolded.

BEEF IT UP

If you think your CV looks a little 'thin' and you have some time to spare, try a few activities to pep it up:

- *IT training*: complete courses in the most up-to-date versions of software.

- *People skills*: work for the university's entertainments committee, chair a club, join a team or band, or be a course representative.

- *Initiative*: do some independent travel or fundraising.

- *Interest in the field of work*: arrange work experience, join occupational bodies as a student member.

- *Responsibility*: mentoring kids, handling money, supervising other people.

- *Communication*: learn another language or write for the university newspaper.

For more CV tips, try *How to Write a Winning CV* by Alan Jones, Random House, £6.99.

THE COVERING LETTER

Many job advertisements ask you to send your CV in with a covering letter. Keep this one-page long, and lively and interesting. Include contact details and address, and mention where and when you saw the advertisement. Use the covering letter to explain why you're interested in the job and what experience you could bring to it. If you're sending your CV as an email attachment, treat your email as the covering letter.

APPLICATION FORMS

Some organisations want you to fill in an application form. Start by photocopying it a couple of times. Read instructions carefully to make sure you're filling it in properly. Practise on one of your photocopies first. Stick to making important points, sound dynamic and keep writing neat. Get someone to check your answers, then fill in the real form carefully. Keep forms clean and uncreased. Keep a photocopy for your records and then return forms by first-class post. If you're sent an application form as an email attachment, fill it in on your computer and use the spell checker.

TESTS AND ASSESSMENTS

Some companies ask applicants to attend testing centres before they will invite them in for a formal interview, as a way of picking out the ideal candidates and narrowing down numbers. Find out well in advance what format the tests will take. Turn up smartly dressed and be polite and pleasant. Your university careers service will have information to help you prepare.

INTERVIEWS

An interview offer means you're in with a serious chance of getting the job. Prepare by:

- **Reviewing advertisements**
- **Reviewing your CV and covering letter**

- **Researching the company**
- **Checking with the employer to see what format the interview will take**
- **Thinking about questions you might be asked**
- **Doing practice interviews**
- **Putting together one or two questions**
- **Smartening your appearance**
- **Reading newspapers**

First impressions are very important. Be dressed correctly and use good non-verbal communication. Find out in advance what most people who work in the organisation wear and go for something similar. Get your hair cut, clean your shoes, iron clothes. The night before, pack your bag with interview letter, CV, employer's contact details, map of their location.

Arrive ten minutes early and smarten up before going in to meet people. When introduced to your interviewers, make eye contact, smile, shake hands firmly and say 'hello'. You'll be invited to take a seat. Sit up straight in your chair and try not to fidget.

Interview formats vary. You may have one interviewer, a series of interviewers or a panel interview. Make eye contact with whoever's talking, but don't stare. Glance at other interviewers from time to time.

Check body language throughout the interview. If your hands get shaky, try folding them loosely on your lap. Sit up straight or lean slightly forwards to look confident and motivated.

Think about your voice. If possible, match it to the speed of the interviewer's delivery. Don't swear or use slang.

The interviewers will probably tell you a few things about the company, ask you some questions about your CV or application form and other general questions. You may also be asked to give a short presentation, talk through some of the items in your portfolio or take an aptitude test.

At the end of the interview, you should be given the chance to ask some questions of your own. Pick one or two good ones that suggest you already know something about the company and would like to know more. When it's all over, shake hands again, and say 'thank you' before you leave. If you don't hear from them within the agreed time, follow it up with a polite phone call. If you don't get the job, ask for feedback.

Read *Perfect Interview* by Max Eggert, Random House £6.99 or *Successful Interview Skills* by Rebecca Corfield, Kogan Page, £7.99.

YOUR BRILLIANT CAREER

If you want a career, as opposed to any old job, you need to know what kind of person you are and what motivates you.

SO, WHO THE HELL ARE YOU?

People who are successful have one thing in common: a sense of purpose. To find your sense of purpose you have to dig deep to work out what makes you tick, then begin to select the types of work that suit your personal style and values. Once you know what you want, you can make a better plan for how you're going to go out and get it. There are many elements to cover, including:

- **Interests**
  Try writing down a list of fifteen things you enjoy doing: underneath the usual 'sex, booze and eating pizza' entries you might find something to work with.

- **Personality**
  The university careers centre has personality tests you can take. Well-known resources used in industry include the Myers-Brigg Type Indicator and the Keirsey Temperament Sorter.

- **Strengths**
  Ask people who know you to write down your greatest strengths. They might value things about you that you were previously unaware of or that you tend to place a lesser importance on.

- **Skills**
  Ability in particular areas can be divided into 'hard' skills and 'soft' skills. Hard skills include IT training, being able to drive a car and so on. Employers are also looking for graduates who can demonstrate well-developed soft skills, such as effective communication, teamwork, negotiation, time management, problem solving and commercial awareness.

- **Values**
  What floats your boat? Is it being independent, having authority, being accepted, doing good deeds for others, high salary or being treated with consideration? Organisations have their own values too.

GO GET THAT JOB!

Make friends with your university careers service early on in your course. They can offer:

- **Testing and interviews to help you find out what type of work might suit you best**

- **A CV service**

- **Books, booklets and leaflets about certain jobs**

- **Lists of vacancies**

- **Detailed advice about local employers**

- **Information about grants, work experience and post-graduate funding**

- **Interview technique lessons**

GATHERING IDEAS

Use the university, job websites or handbooks to find out the range of jobs in interesting areas and begin to narrow it down to a smaller range of job titles.

Research these jobs thoroughly. Find out about qualifications and skills needed, major employers, starting salary and speed of career progression.

Read magazines, newspapers and journals to get a feel for the industry. Attend careers fairs. If you know anyone who works in any of these jobs already, ask them about it.

MOVE INTO ACTION
Prepare a killer CV and tailor it to each job. Find advertised vacancies:

- **On careers centre lists**
- **At your university job shop**
- **In the local job centre**
- **In graduate sections of newspapers**
- **At employment agencies**
- **On graduate employment websites**

Write or email for application forms, or send a CV and covering letter if requested. Many undergraduates start applying for paid employment in their final academic year – apply early and beat the rush.

INCREASE YOUR CHANCES
Milk rounds are days or evenings when employers come to the university to look for the brightest graduates. Take your CV along with you and chat with recruiters to find out as much as you can. Go along to recruitment fairs too, and treat them like mini-interviews.

Make the jobs come to you. Research individual organisations, get in touch with their human resources department or check their website regularly for opportunities. Ring them up and try to find out whether they're hiring soon. Even if they aren't, send your details in.

THE FINAL PHASE
If the interview goes well you will be offered the position and a starting salary. The employer might expect you to ask for more money at this point

and you can negotiate for a little extra if you know the wage is less than the industry standard.

If you have more than one offer on the table, go for the job that's going to meet your needs and give you good long-term prospects. Once you've chosen a particular offer, write back, mentioning the specific title and salary. You may have to meet certain conditions before getting the job, such as passing a medical or getting a certain class of degree. The organisation then sends you a contract to sign, which you should check thoroughly. If you decide to decline an offer, write to them quickly, remembering to say thanks and that you regret you will not be able to take the job. Then all you have to do is start working. See Chapter 10 for Working life.

CHAPTER 8: HEALTH AND STRESS

Sexual health, contraception, alcohol and drug emergencies are covered in Chapter 4, and this chapter covers:

- **Practical and financial help**
- **Keeping yourself healthy**
- **How to spot meningitis**
- **Germs to avoid**
- **Mental and emotional health**
- **Common student ailments and injuries**

HEALTH SERVICES
Large universities usually have a student health centre, experienced in treating problems that commonly affect young people, such as sports injuries, sexual health or mental health. They may also have a dentist and counsellors. Keep the phone number for student health in case of emergencies. Smaller universities offer information about recommended local GPs.

HEALTH BENEFITS
In England and Scotland, full time students under nineteen should get NHS prescriptions, dental treatment and sight tests free. Other students on a low income, or who have chronic medical conditions, should fill in Form HC1 to apply for free or reduced cost prescriptions and other fees. Pick one up from any social security office or most health centres.

WHEN TO CALL AN AMBULANCE (999)

- Someone has been knocked unconscious, even for a few seconds, after an accident or attack

- Heavy bleeding

- Asthma attack

- Anyone might be having, or have had, a fit (seizure)

- Someone is showing possible signs of meningitis (see below for more details)

- Drug-related collapses, fits, violence or extreme paranoia

- Alcohol poisoning

It's also OK to go to casualty if you:

- Need the 'morning after' pill and can't get hold of your GP or a pharmacy that sells it without prescription

- Need emergency dental treatment

If you're unsure, call the NHS Direct Helpline (see Contacts).

STAYING HEALTHY

- **A few useful 'first-aid' items**
  Keep some mild painkillers at home such as paracetamol or ibuprofen, some plasters for cuts and grazes and a tube of antiseptic cream.

- **Screening**
  Checking yourself out regularly can pick up illnesses before they become serious or even life-threatening. For example, everyone should keep an eye out for moles that spread, change colour, itch or bleed. Young men should be particularly aware of testicular cancer, which is relatively easy to cure if it's caught early enough. Get to know the shape and feel of your testicles, and check them out for any new

lumps, bumps and tenderness. Most student health centres have leaflets readily available on how to check yourself. If you do find something, don't let those understandable feelings of fear or embarrassment make you delay visiting the doctor.

On a similar note, young women need to know about breast checks and cervical smears. Check your breasts every month, about a week after the end of your period. Look for tender areas, lumps, tissue thickening, changes in the shape of the breast or nipples and for discharge or bleeding from the nipple.

Depending on your local health authority, you'll be invited for a smear test every three years, either as soon as you reach a certain age (around twenty) or when you tell your GP you're sexually active. It's a very simple procedure, which looks for abnormal changes in cells at the neck of the womb (the cervix). It can be slightly uncomfortable, but is over in a few minutes and gives peace of mind.

- **Eating OK**
  It's hard to eat properly if you're rushing between lectures, part-time jobs and social events. The odd burger or skipped meal isn't going to kill you, but if you're eating junk food regularly you'll feel the effects sooner or later in your wallet, your general health, your skin and your waistline. Eat balanced meals most of the time and drink enough water to keep yourself hydrated, about six to eight glasses per day.

  There's a lot of conflicting advice around about healthy eating. Stick to the basic advice that most nutritionists give: eat five portions of fruit or veg every day, base meals around complex carbohydrates (starchy foods) and have protein in the form of lean meat, fish, eggs, lentils and pulses, or vegetarian alternatives. Moderate your intake of saturated fats and hardened vegetable oil. Don't eat processed, sugary or salty food too often.

- **Sleeping just enough**
  It's part of the deal to have a few late nights partying or sitting up until the small hours doing last-minute work to get an essay in on time.

Have an early night once or twice a week. Sleep deprivation can make you tired, clumsy, unable to concentrate and irritable, and is bad for your health in the longer term. Sleeping too much can also leave you feeling tired and washed out.

- **Keeping fit**
  Regular exercise is good for toning up, increasing stamina and decreasing stress levels. While you're at university, get fit for free, or for a few pounds each term. Most colleges have football pitches, training fields, running tracks and gym facilities, plus various exercise classes.

  If you've never been even remotely fit before then don't worry, it isn't too complicated. Start gently, with about three exercise sessions per week, building up the intensity and length of the sessions over time. Warm up before exerting yourself and warm down with plenty of stretching afterwards. Aim for exercise that makes you feel like you're working and need to breathe more deeply than usual, but stop if you feel wheezy or faint. If you have a medical condition, talk to your doctor before beginning an exercise programme.

- **Smoking**
  In addition to costing hundreds of pounds over the course of a year, cigarettes and roll-ups are bad for your immediate and longer-term health. Being a light smoker is still risky, and smoking cigarettes that are labelled 'light' or 'low tar' is not a safety measure, so don't be fooled. If you want to give up, you have the choice of willpower, nicotine inhalers, nicotine gum, nicotine patches and, as a last resort, prescription drugs from your doctor. Call Quitline: 0800 00 22 00 or ask your local chemist.

BUGS AND GERMS

Most people come down with something sooner or later, and not just the freshers.

COLDS

Most people catch between two and four colds each year, especially during winter. The main symptoms are sneezing and a runny nose. There may also be a sore throat, a bunged-up feeling in the nose and a slight temperature.

Hot drinks, over-the-counter remedies, sore-throat sweets and lashings of daytime TV watched from under a duvet on the sofa all help. To ease congestion, put a towel over your head and inhale steam from a bowl filled with hot water, and avoid smoking.

COUGHS

Coughing is often caused by colds and flu, and other viruses, but it may also be due to allergies or undiagnosed asthma. Try cough mixture from the chemist. Long-lasting coughs need to be checked out by a doctor.

INFLUENZA (FLU)

Flu has a sudden onset, with aches and pains, headache, nausea, runny nose and harsh dry cough. Unlike colds, there is loss of appetite and maybe vomiting or diarrhoea. The illness peaks after two or three days, and the person tends to feel better within a week.

If you catch flu, rest and drink lots of fluids like water, diluted fruit juice or weak tea. Paracetamol or aspirin help with the headache and muscle pains, and can bring the temperature down too. If symptoms last longer than a week, or you start coughing up blood or lots of green phlegm, consult a doctor. If you have asthma or a heart condition, get a flu vaccination every autumn.

GLANDULAR FEVER

Caught from saliva, which is why it's nicknamed 'the kissing disease', and also spread by sneezing. Glandular fever tends to start with one or two weeks of flu-like symptoms. There is enlargement of the lymph nodes ('glands') in the neck, armpits and groin. A very sore throat can develop. There is usually extreme tiredness, muscle pain and sweating. In some people, there may be stomach pains or the liver may be affected. There may be a rash over the body.

Diagnosis is made from blood samples and a throat swab. If confirmed, you need to drink lots of fluids and rest. Most people recover in less than a month. Avoid strenuous activity for at least four weeks after you've started to feel better. If it interferes with your exams, notify the university.

MENINGITIS AND SEPTICAEMIA

Although it's rare, all students should be aware of meningitis because it's so serious. It's an inflammation of the brain and spinal cord, caused by bacteria or viruses. There may also be septicaemia, which is blood poisoning. The symptoms can come on in only a few hours and can vary from person to person. If caught early enough, most people recover, but it can kill.

Look out for **any** of the following:

- **Severe headache**
- **Pain or stiffness in the neck**
- **Dislike of bright lights**
- **Fever and vomiting**
- **Drowsiness or unconsciousness**
- **Stomach cramps or diarrhoea**
- **Signs of septicaemia: tiny red pinprick rash or purplish-red blotches, chills, cold hands and feet. If you press on the blotches with a clear glass tumbler, they do not fade.**

If you suspect meningitis, contact your doctor immediately for advice. If the person is unconscious or having fits, call 999 for an ambulance.

For more information call the Meningitis Research Foundation, tel: 0808 800 3344, or look at www.meningitis.org.uk.

FOOD POISONING

Food poisoning affects about 5.5 million people in the UK each year. It is usually caused by bacteria. If you're preparing food at home, one of the simplest ways to keep down germs is by washing your hands before you cook. Store food at the correct temperature, especially if it's poultry, meat, eggs or fish, and don't use ingredients past their sell by date. Avoid wiping everything in your kitchen down with the same dirty dishcloth.

Be careful when you're eating out, especially late-night kebabs and burgers. Around 10 per cent of fast food is highly contaminated with food- poisoning bacteria. When ordering seafood like mussels, choose busy restaurants that have a fast turnover, and avoid fish on Mondays. Rumours usually abound on campus about a nearby cheapo restaurant or curry house that makes lots of its customers sick. Surprise tip: don't eat there.

Signs of food poisoning vary according to the type of germs involved. There may be violent vomiting within half an hour of eating, fever, chest pain or full-on diarrhoea that starts a while later (hours or even days). Most cases are easy to fight off by taking mild painkillers and drinking lots of fluids, and symptoms are usually gone after three to five days or so. If you can't keep water down, are in severe pain, pass bloody diarrhoea or have violent diarrhoea for more than 24 hours, call your GP.

MENTAL HEALTH

The late teens and early twenties are a common age for people to experience mental-health problems for the first time. There is a wide range of support available.

DEPRESSION

Around one in nine people experience some form of depression, and students may be even more at risk with life stresses like leaving home, relationship breakdowns or serious money problems.

SIGNS AND SYMPTOMS

Depression can have classic signs such as feeling miserable for long periods of time, but also presents in less obvious ways. The list below covers some of the various signs and symptoms:

- **Feeling down, miserable or tearful most days for more than two weeks.**

- **Difficulty sleeping, waking early, having nightmares.**

- **Becoming withdrawn.**

- **Feeling hollow, empty, bored, unable to see a future.**

- **Lack of sex drive, general tiredness.**

- **Thinking about suicide.**

- **Feeling guilty, ashamed, worthless.**

- **Loss of appetite or excessive comfort eating.**

- **Feelings of anger, restlessness, frustration.**

WHAT HELP IS AVAILABLE?

There's a range of medical treatments for depression and a number of self-help techniques. If it's hard to talk about your feelings, try writing it down for your GP or get a friend to come along for moral support. Your doctor can then offer you tests and treatments, or refer you for counselling or other help.

You may be offered antidepressants to even out low levels of brain chemicals such as serotonin. They can take between two and four weeks to have a positive effect. Follow instructions on the packet, don't stop taking them suddenly without talking to your doctor and don't mix with alcohol or street drugs.

Counselling can be very effective, especially if you have unresolved issues from your past or have had painful recent events.

There are also things you can do to help yourself, such as taking regular exercise, eating healthily and getting back to the activities that you enjoy doing. A number of support groups exist for people who have depression or depressed friends or relatives.

Thoughts of suicide should be taken seriously. Go to a doctor as soon as you can, and if you need to talk to someone while you're waiting for the appointment, don't be scared to call the Samaritans. They're open day and night for anyone who is feeling down or has reached a crisis point. If you think a friend is seriously depressed or suicidal, be as supportive as you can, and help them to get medical attention.

ANXIETY AND STRESS
Student life can be much harder than people imagine. It's not surprising that students can end up feeling anxious, overwhelmed or stressed out.

SIGNS AND SYMPTOMS
- **Things feeling out of control.**

- **Lying awake worrying, difficulty sleeping.**

- **Feeling that something bad is about to happen.**

- **Dry mouth, feeling shaky, sweaty palms.**

- **Increased need to pass urine, diarrhoea.**

- **Difficulty concentrating.**

- **Feeling tense and miserable.**

- **Panic attacks: sweating, dizziness, racing heartbeat, difficulty breathing or a sense of impending doom or death.**

- **Phobias: irrational fears of things or situations, such as crowded places, blood, spiders, birds or heights.**

- **Obsessions and compulsions: ritual behaviour that's usually carried out to cope with unpleasant thoughts.**

WHAT HELP IS AVAILABLE?

Some stress is normal in everyday life, but specific measures are sometimes needed to reduce it. Getting it all off your chest can be helpful, whether that's talking to a friend, relative or counsellor.

Stress or anxiety may be a sign that you need to make some alterations to your behaviour and lifestyle. Most universities run free stress-reduction courses and relaxation sessions, where you can learn simple but effective techniques that will help you to be calmer in a variety of situations. Many people also say that exercise such as yoga or swimming can be very relaxing, or that meditation helps. Avoiding caffeine can reduce feelings of jitteriness.

If you have strong feelings of anxiety or panic, try the following:

- **Concentrate on your breathing and take long, slow breaths in and out.**

- **If possible, sit somewhere quiet while you calm yourself down.**

- **Tell yourself that your anxious thoughts are creating these feelings and that you can get in control of these thoughts.**

- **Focus your attention onto something else, away from your feelings.**

If anxieties, phobias or obsessions are affecting your daily life, it's best to get to the bottom of them. Your doctor will be able to provide you with explanations and reassurance, and give you a thorough check-up to rule out any other underlying illness. They can also teach you about relaxation techniques or refer you to a specialist for further treatment such as counselling or psychological help.

MANIC DEPRESSION AND SCHIZOPHRENIA

Manic depression and schizophrenia each affect around 1 per cent of the adult population, and can show up for the first time in the teens or twenties. They are often confusing or frightening for the people concerned and those who know them. There may be a family history, and episodes of illness can be brought on by stress.

SIGNS AND SYMPTOMS: SCHIZOPHRENIA

- A feeling that thoughts are being controlled by someone else.

- Hearing voices, e.g. being talked about.

- Giving extraordinary meanings to ordinary events (delusions).

- Conversation that lacks logical flow or contains made-up words.

- Hallucinations.

- Becoming withdrawn, not coping with everyday living activities.

- Flat moods, where there is little up or down.

SIGNS AND SYMPTOMS: MANIC DEPRESSION

- Swinging between symptoms of depression and mania (see the symptoms below).

- Increased feelings of energy, self-esteem, self-confidence and restlessness.

- Embarking on reckless behaviour, such as spending vast sums of money.

- Sleeping very little, not feeling tired.

- Rushed speaking and thinking, not making much sense.

- Acting self-important, or believing things that aren't true.

WHAT HELP IS AVAILABLE?

The main treatment for manic depression and schizophrenia is drugs and social support, such as regular visits from community psychiatric nurses. Anti-psychotic medications reduce hallucinations and delusions. If someone is in the acute phase of either illness, they are usually admitted to hospital. In the depressive phase of manic depression, antidepressants are often prescribed, and they may also be given mood-stabilising drugs such as lithium. Many only have one or two episodes of illness, and others find their symptoms are controlled well by drugs.

EATING DISORDERS

Eating disorders include anorexia nervosa, bulimia nervosa and compulsive eating. They all have a distorted attitude to food in common, where emotional needs drive eating behaviour, rather than hunger. Nine out of ten sufferers are female.

ANOREXIA NERVOSA

It's thought that 1 per cent of teenage girls suffer from anorexia, and 5 per cent of girls and young women show symptoms to a lesser degree. It's characterised by:

- **Deliberate weight loss, over 15 per cent below your healthy body weight.**

- **Intense fear of being fat or desperate wish to be thin.**

- **Loss of periods for three months or more in females.**

- **Placing all self-worth on weight and appearance.**

- **There may also be laxative abuse or excessive exercise.**

Sufferers may have perfectionist tendencies or difficulty expressing their needs or feelings. Severe weight loss causes tiredness, faintness and dizziness, and an emaciated appearance. There may be constipation, stomach pains and hair loss. There can also be a growth of fine downy hair all over the body and a constant feeling of coldness. Over time, anorexia may cause osteoporosis (thinning of the bones) and damage to the heart, and depression and anxiety are common.

BULIMIA NERVOSA

Bulimia is most common among women in their late teens and early twenties. It can be recognised by the following:

- **Recurrent episodes of binge-eating, where large quantities of rich or sugary food are consumed quickly, usually in secret.**

- **Lack of control over the amount eaten during a binge.**
- **Weight usually within normal limits.**
- **After a binge, attempts to lose weight again by vomiting, purging with laxatives, fasting or strict dieting.**

Bulimics may feel that they are worthless, despite being popular or high achievers, and sometimes have a history of dieting or being obese as a child. Regular vomiting can damage teeth. It can also cause bleeding in the throat and dangerous disturbances in the balance of the body's fluid and mineral levels. Long-term laxative abuse leads to constipation and bloating.

COMPULSIVE EATING
Probably the most common eating disorder, where the person consumes large amounts of food by bingeing or snacking throughout the day. It may be an extreme form of comfort eating. Men are more likely to have problems with compulsive eating than with anorexia or bulimia.

RECOVERING FROM EATING DISORDERS
If you think you may have an eating disorder, the sooner you seek help, the better. Start by speaking to a doctor or nurse, or one of the organisations listed in the box below. Treatment includes changing to a healthier eating pattern to get to a normal weight, various types of therapy and antidepressant drugs.

SELF-HARM
Sufferers deliberately harm themselves, most often secretly, as a temporary way of coping with unhappy or unpleasant feelings. This can take the form of cutting the skin, picking or bruising the skin, pulling out hair, taking small overdoses and so on. Treatment is a course of counselling, designed to bring personal problems out into the open and provide healthier ways of coping with negative feelings and stress.

USEFUL CONTACTS AND RESOURCES FOR MENTAL HEALTH

MIND

Leading mental health charity with information, local support and campaigns.

Infoline: 0845 766 0163, website: www.mind.org.uk

DEPRESSION ALLIANCE

A charity dedicated to helping people understand and recover from depression.

Telephone: 020 7633 0557, website: www.depressionalliance.org

EATING DISORDERS ASSOCIATION

Information and help on all aspects of eating disorders.

Adult helpline: 0845 634 1414, open 8.30 a.m.–8.30 p.m., Monday to Friday
Youthline: 0845 634 7650, open 4 p.m.–6.30 p.m., Monday to Friday

Minicom: 01603 753322, open 8.30 a.m.–8.30 p.m., Monday to Friday

NO PANIC

Confidential help and rehabilitation for anyone suffering from anxiety, phobias or obsessive compulsive disorder.

Helpline: 0808 808 0545, open 10 a.m.–10 p.m. daily, website: www.nopanic.org.uk

CRUSE

Information and advice for people who are bereaved.

Helpline: 020 8940 4818, open 9.30 a.m.–5 p.m., Monday to Friday

BRISTOL CRISIS CENTRE

Service dedicated to helping women who self-harm, helpline covers the whole of the UK.

Helpline: 0117 925 1119, open 9 p.m.–12.30 a.m., Friday and Saturday, and 6 p.m.–9 p.m. Sunday

SAMARITANS

Confidential service for anyone who is suicidal or despairing.

Telephone: 08457 90 90 90 (UK), 1850 60 90 90 (Republic of Ireland), email: jo@samaritans.org

OTHER COMMON HEALTH PROBLEMS

SKIN TROUBLE

ACNE
Hormone changes, increased oil production, stress, dead skin cells, inflammation and bacteria all gang up on your skin to give you acne or zits. Wash skin gently and regularly, and don't pick it. For mild acne try products containing benzoyl peroxide, salicylic acid or tea tree oil, and expect improvement after around one month. For moderate acne your GP can prescribe antibiotics, or for women a certain brand of the contraceptive pill may work. If acne is severe, get referred to a dermatologist.

ECZEMA
Areas of skin affected by eczema become very dry, itchy, and flaky. It can also be reddened, sore, inflamed or weepy. It tends to affect areas such as the elbows, wrists, hands, face, and backs of the knees. The itchiness can keep people awake, and make them feel irritable, plus certain foods and stress can make it worse. Stop the skin from drying out, use soapless cleansers and emollient (moisturising) creams and lotions. Corticosteroid creams and antihistamines may work too; ask the chemist.

PSORIASIS
Psoriasis sometimes starts during the teenage years after sore throats, chest infections or stress. It sometimes runs in families and isn't contagious. Rapid cell turnover causes 'plaques' where skin is thicker. Plaques are itchy red or dark-pink areas, with a scaly surface, commonly on knees, ankles and scalp. There are several products to get rid of plaques: Vitamin D-like creams, steroids, coal tar and ultraviolet-light treatment. Keeping skin moisturised reduces itching.

HAY FEVER
Allergic reaction to grass, flower or tree pollens affects up to one in five students. Try antihistamines, nasal sprays and eye drops. Reducing contact

with pollen keeps symptoms down: close windows, wear sunglasses to protect eyes, etc. If symptoms go on all year, it's probably allergies to dust mites or pets.

ASTHMA

Asthma is a long-term condition affecting the breathing, ranging from mild wheeziness to full-blown asthma attacks. The lining of the smallest airways in the lungs becomes inflamed and the muscles in the walls of the airways may contract, causing the airways to become narrowed. Can be made worse by cold, exercise, cigarette smoke, viruses or specific substances such as certain foods. Sometimes there is no wheezing, just coughing at night.

A severe asthma attack needs urgent medical attention. Signs of an attack are: bluish skin or lips and gasping breath, restlessness, confusion or a drawn-in ribcage. Using inhalers regularly and monitoring the asthma tend to be the most effective ways to manage the condition. If you know you have asthma, make sure you're registered with a GP and always have enough inhalers.

SPORTS INJURIES

To reduce the risk of sports injuries, warm up fully when exercising, use the right protective equipment and warm down gently afterwards. Injuries include bruising, sprained tendons and broken bones. If you're injured don't soldier on, get off the pitch before you make it worse. An ice pack or bag of frozen peas may help to bring swelling down while you wait for the doctor or X-ray technician. If you do contact sports, be aware of the possibility of facial, head, neck and back injuries. Never move someone with a suspected injury of this type until qualified help arrives, unless the person is choking and you have to clear their airway. Treatment for most sport injuries includes rest, painkillers, strapping or other support, physiotherapy and anti-inflammatory drugs.

OBESITY

Carrying extra weight can worsen existing health conditions and increases risk of high blood pressure and heart disease. Get weighed properly by the nurse at your health centre, find out if you really do need to lose a few pounds and ask for a healthy eating plan. Get down to your recommended weight slowly and take regular exercise, to make sure it doesn't go back on again.

RELIABLE SOURCES OF HEALTH INFORMATION

NHS DIRECT
Advice helpline staffed by trained nurses, plus a website containing comprehensive, easy to understand advice.

Telephone: 0845 46 47, open 24 hours daily, website: www.nhsdirect.nhs.uk

NETDOCTOR.CO.UK
The UK's leading independent health website, with drug and illness encyclopaedias, message boards and an email query service.

CHAPTER 9: CRIME AND SAFETY

One-third of students have been the victims of crime in the last twelve months, a sobering statistic. The most common crimes are burglary and other robbery, and criminal damage.

If you see a crime taking place, find someone who has been attacked or injured or you think you're in danger, call 999 quickly. To report petty theft or other similar crimes, contact your local police station directly.

All students should be aware of:

- **Burglaries**
- **Street or campus crime**
- **Safety at night**
- **Harassment and sexual assault**
- **Their rights if stopped by police**

Everyone at university should get their possessions insured. All insurance policies require you to take reasonable care of your own property, and some of them insist you fulfil certain conditions, such as fitting specific locks to your bedroom or front door.

SAFETY AT HOME

Many thefts are opportunistic, with burglars using open windows or doors in about a quarter of robberies. Being careful about who you let in, remembering to lock up regularly and taking a few security measures, reduces your chances of being burgled.

ACCESS
If you live in halls or shared flats and somebody turns up claiming to be visiting another student, find out exactly who they are looking for, then go and get the student in question to see if it's a wanted visitor. Chancers may ring the buzzer and say they're looking for 'Dave' or 'Mike', or claim to be from a utilities company or 'sent by the landlord'. Ask to see proper identification and call the company if necessary. Get them to put their ID card through the letterbox.

HALL SAFETY
Leaving your hall room unattended while you shower or make a cup of tea could allow a sneak thief to grab your personal belongings or give an attacker enough time to hide in your room to await your return. When letting yourself into entry halls, shut the door firmly behind you.

LOCKING UP
Always lock up whenever you leave your room or house. If you live in a shared house or flat, check around before you go out or off to bed, making sure doors are locked and windows closed. Lock garden gates.

SECURITY MEASURES
- If you're thinking about renting a place, pick one with sturdy doors, strong locks and secure windows, preferably with a burglar alarm.

- Nag landlords to provide decent locks on the front door and bedroom doors, a door chain and window locks.

- A visible burglar alarm can be a deterrent.

- Try not to display valuables near your windows.

- If you're leaving your house unattended during the holidays, put valuables in secure storage, take them with you or leave them with trustworthy friends. Ask friendly neighbours to keep an eye on the place and leave a contact phone number with them.

- **Mark expensive items with an invisible UV pen. If goods are stolen, there's a chance police will be able to return them.**

- **Don't leave spare door keys outside under the doormat or in a nearby plant pot. It's the first place a burglar will look.**

ON THE STREET OR ON CAMPUS

Don't flash around cash, mobile phones or laptops in the street, it could make you a target for theft. Don't leave purses, wallets or bags unattended, even for a brief moment. Unattended coats are frequently stolen because of what they might have in their pockets, so look after your jacket.

YOUR BAGS AND WALLET

Clear your bag out regularly and only take what you need out with you. Don't keep your cheque card and chequebook in the same bag or jacket. Avoid keeping your keys in the same bag as letters or bills with your home address on them, to prevent burglary. Don't put your wallet or purse in the back pocket of your jeans; it's safer in an inside or zipped pocket.

MOBILE PHONES

When you're out, keep your phone tucked away and be careful answering calls in the street. Write the SIM card serial number down and keep it in a safe place at home – it can be used to block the phone and stop the thief from making calls at your expense. Report the theft of your phone to your service provider and the police as soon as you can.

CASH TILLS

Never write card PINs down and don't tell other people the number. Use cashpoints in daylight if you can and look out for people standing too close while you're taking money out. Make sure nobody sees you entering your PIN and don't count your money in the street.

OUT AT NIGHT

When you're going out, tell someone where you're going. Plan how you're getting home – if possible book a taxi before you go out. Some student unions have a free night safety bus or recommend a taxi firm. Get a personal attack alarm and know how to use it to disorientate an assailant so you can get away.

Know your limits if you're drinking and remember alcohol affects your judgement. Don't let friends wander off on their own drunk or on drugs, and don't let anyone walk home alone. Never leave drinks unattended.

If you do meet a problem, your aim should be to get away. Trust your instincts and start running for a place where you know there are people. Physical defence is a last resort. Report incidents quickly even if you were unharmed; you may save someone else.

GETTING HOME SAFELY

Avoid walking home alone at night if possible. If you are out alone, try to walk with a group of people, preferably a mixed group of males and females. Avoid poorly lit areas. Walk quickly and confidently, facing oncoming traffic, and carry an attack alarm in your hand if you have one.

- **Only 'black cab' taxis can be hailed in the street.**

- **Never get into an unlicensed or unmarked minicab that pulls up beside you – it's illegal and possibly dangerous.**

- **Keep the number of a trusted cab company with you and, when booking, ask for the driver's name.**

- **Confirm the driver's details when the cab arrives and sit in the back of the car, not the front.**

- **When using public transport, know departure times of last trains, tubes and buses.**

- **Have ticket, pass or change ready, keeping purse or wallet out of sight, and wait in a well-lit place, near other people if possible.**

- **Sit near emergency alarms.**

- **Sit downstairs near the driver on buses.**

- **On tubes or trains, avoid empty carriages.**

- **Speak to the driver if someone is bothering you and make sure they can't follow you off the bus or train.**

- **Don't hitch-hike.**

VIOLENCE

In some towns there may be 'student bashing' where locals attack students. Stick to student-friendly pubs and bars or ask older students about places to avoid in town. Drunken fights and muggings are also common, often near pubs and clubs at night after victims have been drinking, so take care when leaving places. If somebody is trying to take your bag or mobile, let it go.

HELPING OTHERS

If you see someone else in trouble, think for a second before going to their aid. If you're on your own, you could be outnumbered or facing an armed attacker. You may help more by alerting the police or university security. If you see someone lying in the street who looks as though they've been attacked or injured, your priority is to make sure the attackers are no longer around before you offer help. Someone who has been robbed or attacked may be in shock, so speak gently to them and call for help if they look pale and shaky. Put a coat over their shoulders. If you find someone who has been glassed, leave glass in the wound and call 999. If someone has been stabbed, press the sides of the wound together while you're waiting for the ambulance. The knife may have been left in – don't try to remove it and be careful not to get cut. Try not to move anyone who looks like they've been badly beaten or hit by a car, unless they are not breathing. If someone is drunk and has been beaten or mugged, get medical attention even if they want to go home – they could have been hurt more than they realise.

CARS, MOTORBIKES AND BICYCLES

A few tips:

- Park in well-lit, busy places.

- If you want to park on campus, set off early. Spaces are limited.

- Remove the car stereo and take it with you.

- Lock the car up properly every time you leave it, even if it's only for a brief period.

- Get a steering-wheel lock, an immobiliser, or electronic alarm.

- Don't keep vehicle registration documents, cash or credit cards in the glove compartment, or valuables in view.

- Buy a D-lock for bicycles and attach to something sturdy.

- Get a security number etched onto your bike frame.

CARD FRAUD

Keep a note of card numbers and emergency card-theft hotlines at home in case your wallet gets stolen. Don't let cards out of your sight during transactions in shops or restaurants in case they get 'skimmed' (someone runs your card through a tiny reader, then the number is used to obtain goods without your knowledge). Report stolen cards to the issuer immediately. When internet shopping, use reputable established websites with secure services and never put your full card number into an email. Check statements every month for unexpected purchases and query any strange items, no matter how small.

SAFETY FOR MEN

Men are twice as likely to be subjected to a violent attack as women. You don't need to fit into the stereotype of being tough or heroic, in fact this can make some situations worse. Physical self-defence is a last resort. It limits your options and commits you to a fight you could lose. It is not weak to walk away – you don't have to prove anything to yourself or others.

RAPE AND SEXUAL ASSAULT

Both men and women can become the victims of rape or sexual assault.

AVOIDING ACQUAINTANCE RAPE

A Home Office study found that only 8 per cent of rapes were carried out by strangers. Women were most at risk from current partners, former partners, men they were dating and their acquaintances.

- **If you are meeting someone new, tell friends where you're going, who you're meeting, and when you expect to return. If your plans change, tell someone.**

- **Arrange your first meeting with someone in a busy public place, preferably in daylight.**

- **If it's a blind date, take a friend along with you who can watch and wait nearby. Take a mobile phone.**

- **Trust your instincts – if someone makes you nervous or uneasy leave immediately.**

- **Don't drink too much alcohol. Be aware of drink spiking.**

AFTER AN ATTACK

If someone has been raped or sexually assaulted, or thinks they may have been drugged and attacked, they may be in shock and will need medical help. They have the right to go to the police and report the attack, if they want the attacker to be prosecuted. If so they should go to the police as soon as they can, taking a friend or counsellor along for support if possible. Keeping on the clothes they were wearing and avoiding showering is necessary to preserve evidence. The trauma can affect people differently and may bring up strong feelings of shame, guilt, disgust or anger. This may happen immediately or after a long or short delay. Support from an organisation such as Rape Crisis or Survivors can be extremely helpful, no matter how long ago or how recently the attack took place. Rape Crisis exists to help any woman who has been raped or sexually assaulted;

telephone 0115 900 3560, 9 a.m.–5.30 p.m. on weekdays to find out the details of the nearest Rape Crisis Centre or look in the local phone book.

MALE RAPE
Research suggests that the primary motivation behind male rape is not to release sexual frustration but to humiliate and destroy. Many victims feel too traumatised or ashamed to seek help. Male rape victims still need to seek medical attention, and have the right to report the attack to the police, get their attacker prosecuted and have counselling. Survivors is set up to help male rape victims and their helpline is 020 7833 3737.

HARASSMENT
It is illegal to threaten or pester another person, including making nuisance phone calls, stalking, and homophobic or racist behaviour. Your local police station should be your first port of call if you wish to complain or ask for protection.

MALICIOUS PHONE CALLS
If you get a malicious call, stay calm and don't make any response. Put the handset down and walk away. If calls persist, unplug your landline or switch off your mobile for a while. Contact your phone provider for more advice.

STALKING
Stalking is persistent unwanted attention and affects around 3 per cent of students. It may take the form of death threats or being followed everywhere, or someone may send unwanted notes, love letters or gifts. Stalking victims live in chronic fear, which takes its toll. If you think you are being stalked, go to the local police.

Tell family, friends, neighbours and people at work what is going on and ask them to look out for you. Do not agree to meet your stalker, and if you do see them show as little emotion as possible. Make a note of any incidents, and if anything arrives in the post don't handle it – place in a plastic bag to preserve fingerprints or other evidence. Get a mobile phone, a personal alarm and improve your home security. You can engage a solicitor to take out a restraining order. Victim Support and the Suzy Lamplugh Trust can provide more information.

USEFUL NUMBERS

VICTIM SUPPORT

An organisation that exists to help all victims of crime. They can help by offering counselling, practical advice and support to witnesses in court. You can telephone their Victim Supportline on 0845 30 30 900. It's open 9 a.m.–9 p.m. Monday to Friday, 9 a.m.–7 p.m. weekends and 9 a.m.–5 p.m. bank holidays. There's also a minicom (or text telephone) number on 020 7896 3776, and a website at www.victimsupport.com.

THE SUZY LAMPLUGH TRUST

This organisation has provided much of the information in the personal safety section of this chapter. They are the leading UK safety advice charity and can be contacted for more information by writing to them at: National Centre for Personal Safety, Hampton House, 20 Albert Embankment, London SE1 7TJ, telephoning 020 7091 0014, or via their website: www.suzylamplugh.org.

YOU AND THE LAW

If police stop you in the street, you have to give them your name and address if asked. You don't have to answer any other questions there and then if you don't want to, but you could be arrested if you refuse. You have a right to ask why they've stopped you. Be courteous and move along if they ask. In public, they can only check through your outer clothing and the search should be done by an officer of the same sex as you.

The police may ask you to accompany them down to the station. You can refuse but they can then arrest you if they suspect you're connected to a crime. Should you be arrested, you have the right to know exactly what for and the police have to provide a written copy of your legal rights. You must also be allowed to see a duty solicitor, which is a free service, or your own solicitor if you have one. Wait until the solicitor arrives before answering any police questions. You can also have one other person notified that you've been arrested. Once you've been arrested, the police can search, fingerprint and photograph you. If you're not charged with an offence, these records must be destroyed afterwards.

Anyone who thinks they have been treated unfairly by the police can make a complaint. If you are at the police station ask to see the duty inspector, who will tell you how to make your complaint formal.

CHAPTER 10: GRADUATION AND BEYOND

All good things must come to an end, but as graduation looms and your time as an undergraduate draws to a close, you might be able to line up something even better.

This chapter looks at

- **Graduation and getting your certificates**
- **Making the most of graduate jobs**
- **Employment options and work searches**
- **Graduate study and funding**
- **Post-university gap years**

WHAT GRADUATING IS REALLY LIKE

After final-year exams, your department tells you in advance when the results will be announced. If you got the results you wanted, celebrate! If things didn't go so well, contact your course tutors to talk through what went wrong and whether or not resits are needed.

Once you know you're going to be graduating, decide whether or not to attend the ceremony. Many students say this event is more of a 'thank you' to their parents than anything else, and if they've helped to put you through university then it's a kind gesture to make.

THE GRAND CEREMONY

Formal graduation ceremonies require you to dress in hired university robes and caps, preferably with something smart on underneath. Some token details about gown and cap size are taken, but rest assured it's always a loose-fitting unflattering garment.

Presentations take place in a large hall, overseen by the university's chancellor. The whole ceremony can take hours because of all the speeches and the number of graduates. Even if you're bored silly, your parents will probably be loving it and may insist on having your picture taken by a professional photographer afterwards. Some universities then lay on a party or a formal lunch or dinner for the new graduates and their guests. If you don't go to your graduation ceremony, make arrangements to graduate 'in absentia' – sign a form to say you won't be there and get your degree certificate sent by post.

COMMON CHOICES FOR NEW GRADUATES

At the moment, among students who have just graduated:

- **33 per cent go straight into a graduate job**
- **29 per cent take a holiday or gap year**
- **23 per cent are looking for a graduate job**
- **20 per cent go straight to further study**
- **17 per cent take temporary jobs**

(figures from the UNITE and MORI Student Living Report)

If you don't have anything lined up or you're still not sure what you want to do, don't despair. You don't have to decide immediately.

STARTING YOUR GRADUATE JOB

Before your first day, look through all the literature your new employer has provided. Check your contract to see whether or not you have a probation period and what targets you have to meet within it. Be on your best behaviour for its duration. Turn up looking smart on your first day and know where you're going and when. You should then have an induction.

Inductions can vary. If you're lucky you get a welcome pack, training, a supervisor to contact if you're stuck and orientation for the whole building.

Whatever happens in your first few days, make the best of it, and keep a note of everything important such as names, departments, phone numbers and codes.

Be polite and friendly to everyone, even if they seem a bit distant or grumpy. Don't be scared to say that you're new and you don't know where something is. Volunteer to do a few things such as make the coffee or take files to a different floor – get your face seen. Beware of office gossip and the office lech, and make a few friends you can go down the pub with after the end of the working day. Do your best to remember people's names, and if you're having trouble look at photo boards in reception or the company website.

The first few weeks can be unsettling and tiring. If you're mostly doing menial tasks such as filing or data inputting, don't worry too much at the beginning. Do tasks well and on time, then start asking for more responsibility or training. If the work doesn't get any more interesting after the first few weeks, speak to your supervisor about your expectations for the job, to see if anything can be done.

Once you've settled into the job, think about how it matches up with your career aspirations. Is it worth staying and finding out how easy it is to rise through the ranks or should you step up to a better position by moving to a different organisation? Every six months or so, make a mental check of what you have learned or otherwise gained from your current job, and set some modest targets for the next six months. Keep an eye on the employment market to see how your current work matches up and what your other options are.

STILL LOOKING FOR A GRADUATE JOB?

Thousands of graduates leave university without a 'proper' job to go to. Stay in touch with the university careers centre over the summer and beyond, keeping an eye on their job lists and looking for employers. Treat your job search as if it was a type of employment itself. Get up on time and plan your week around finding something.

Consider the following:

- **Broadening the subject areas or types of work you could try.**

- **Visiting careers centres and job centres more regularly.**

- **Reviewing CV and interview technique.**

- **Newspapers' graduate sections.**

- **Voluntary work or work experience.**

- **Checking local businesses, newspapers or shop windows.**

- **Talking to everyone you know about your search.**

- **Signing up with all job websites that have suitable vacancies, and using their full range of facilities.**

- **Try advice websites such as www.prospects.ac.uk or www.doctorjob.com.**

- **Introducing yourself to graduate recruitment agencies.**

- **Being flexible about location or salary.**

- **Taking on a stopgap job or part-time work.**

- **Keeping your job searching records in a neat file.**

If you're unemployed when your course ends, visit the employment job centre quickly with your national insurance number, have a new jobseeker interview and sign on for Jobseeker's Allowance (JSA). Apply for anything else you're eligible for, such as housing benefit, getting independent advice from your local Citizen Advice Bureau if necessary. Most job centres make you turn up fortnightly to sign on and ask for proof you've been actively seeking work. This is where keeping a file of your records comes in handy – it keeps benefits officers off your back. Find out more about benefits at www.dwp.gov.uk.

Anyone who is unemployed and has serious debts should take a long hard look at their finances. If you're earning less than £15,000 per year, you won't have to make student loan repayments, so don't worry about them. However, if you owe money on credit cards, loans or overdrafts, then you need to make a plan. If you can't borrow money from family to clear some or all of these debts, then write to your creditors to explain your situation, preferably before you start missing payments. Say that you're currently job-hunting and hopeful, and would like to discuss ways to repay the money more slowly. Once you do find work, throw as much money at your high-interest debts as you can. See debt information in Chapter 6.

TAKING A STOPGAP JOB OR TEMPING

A stopgap job is anything that helps you pay the bills, from stacking shelves in Woolworth's to pulling pints down the local. Temping has more potential than most stopgap jobs: can pay fairly well, gives you variety and could allow you to work in your chosen field. If you are friendly and hard working, the employer may take you on permanently. Sign up with reputable temp agencies that place workers in the area you're interested in and ring them daily sounding keen. Keep building on your skills and soon you'll be able to command higher daily rates. Some agencies offer subsidised training or free online courses.

Agencies are paid for placing you in any old job. Don't get pushed into doing stuff you know you'll hate, unless it's your first job with a new agency and you want to get your foot in the door. Check your agency is paying you the correct going rate. Strike up a rapport with one of the recruitment staff, so they help you find the best jobs.

BECOMING YOUR OWN BOSS

Perhaps you aren't cut out for working for other people or you have a brilliant idea for a business. If that's the case, think about becoming self-employed or freelance.

Benefits of being self-employed:

- **Freedom of running your own company**

- **Sense of achievement**
- **Potential earnings can be very high**

The downside of being self-employed:

- **Companies may delay paying you**
- **Need to keep good records and sort out tax**
- **Long hours, lots of responsibility**
- **Most new businesses fail within two years**

To start your own business successfully you need a detailed plan and extensive research. Identify a market for your services or products. You don't need a unique service or idea, start by looking at companies doing well in the area you're interested in. Carry out market research to work out whether there's sufficient demand for your skills or goods.

If your idea is likely to sell, you will probably need some start-up money to help you get going: money for premises, equipment, stock, staff, training, insurance and so on. This can come from savings, bank loans, small business support networks, venture capital or grants. Think hard about marketing your business; you won't get any work if nobody's heard about you. You also have to register as self-employed with the Inland Revenue and pay taxes.

Organisations providing free help and advice

The National Federation of Enterprise Agencies (www.nfea.com) is a non-profit independent network of agencies committed to helping small businesses start up and grow. The Prince's Trust provides people aged 18 to 30 with support from a business mentor and makes small grants. Telephone: 0800 842 842, website: www.princes-trust.org.uk. Shell LiveWIRE (www.shell-livewire.org) helps young people aged 16 to 30 to start and develop their own business and hosts a national competition.

POSTGRADUATE STUDY

Around 400,000 students per year enrol to take further university study. It's intensive and can be an enormous financial strain. It can be a way into a career in academia or a prerequisite for certain careers outside academia.

WHY DO POSTGRADUATE STUDY?

- **To learn more about a subject**

- **To improve your career prospects (make sure it's the right qualification for your industry, and your institution is recognised)**

- **Because it's required for your chosen job**

- **To convert to another subject area**

TYPES OF COURSE

Postgraduate courses are broadly split into research-based and taught courses.

Research-based courses:

- **Doctorates: PhD or DPhil. A PhD takes three to four years of full-time study or around five to six years part time. You're expected to carry out original research, write a thesis of around 100,000 words and complete a *viva voce* (spoken) presentation at the end of it.**

- **MPhil: similar structure to doctorates, but have a shorter course (two years or so full time) and a shorter thesis.**

- **Masters: MSc, MA, MRes. Research degrees that take twelve months or so to complete and involve writing a short thesis. Many students who take Masters courses go on to do PhDs in similar subjects.**

Taught courses:

- **Masters: MSc, MA, MBA. These are in the sciences, the arts or business administration. They can last one or two whole years full** time, or two to three years on a part-time basis. They include a mixture of lectures and tutorials, practical experience, research and a thesis, essays and exams.

- **Postgraduate diplomas and certificates:** last around nine months and can be vocational training or conversion courses.

- **PGCE:** the most common type of teacher training. Includes classroom experience, lesson preparation and exams.

- **Professional qualifications:** may be taken at the same time as holding down a job or doing other postgraduate courses such as diplomas.

HOW TO FIND COURSES AND APPLY

Start by talking to staff in your department to see if they think you're suitable and look at information websites such as www.prospects.ac.uk. Your university careers centre should also help. They can show you postgraduate directories, information booklets, books of current research programmes in Britain and postgraduate prospectuses for UK universities. You might be able to attend a postgraduate study fair.

When you've narrowed it down to a type of course and a subject area, gather detailed information about individual departments and courses. Use national newspapers and websites such as www.prospects.ac.uk to find out course details. Specialist magazines and journals such as *Prospects Today*, *Hobsons Postgraduate Update* and *New Scientist* are another good source of places. Look out for salaried academic posts such as research assistantships.

Check for requirements, closing dates and contact details. Ring course organisers up or arrange a visit. Ask the following:

- **Does this institution have a good reputation? How do they score in their official Research Assessment Exercise gradings?**

- **Is the qualification well regarded in the UK? And internationally?**

- **How are you going to fund yourself?**

- **What's the surrounding area like?**

- **What happens to graduates who complete this course? Do they go on to well-paid jobs and cutting edge research?**

- **Is there a thriving postgraduate community?**

- **Will your proposed supervisor be able to teach, support and inspire you?**

Ideally start looking at research degrees one or two years before you are due to finish your undergraduate studies. The best time to apply for places and funding is about a year to six months before courses are due to begin, but don't worry if you've left it later than this. Many courses have places left or you can apply for the following year. Postgraduate degrees don't have a closing date for applications, unless they have a taught component to their timetable, such as some Masters and PGCEs.

Expect to be interviewed by more than one member of staff, usually the proposed supervisor and perhaps the head of department. Brush up on basic research techniques before you go and read around the subject area, including topical items in the news or in the relevant subject journals.

Teacher training information can be obtained from the government's Teacher Training Agency, Portland House, Stag Place, London SW1E 5TT, telephone: 0845 6000 991, website: www.tda.gov.uk.

FUNDING IN THE UK

Postgraduate students need money for fees and living expenses. Your department may help with funding from a number of sources, but also think about finding your own from bodies such as:

- **Research councils (e.g. EPSRC, MRC)**

- **The Arts and Humanities Research Board**

- **The Student Awards Agency for Scotland**

- **Charities, foundations and trusts**

- **Employer sponsorship**

- **Local education authorities (teacher training)**

Full-time students may be able to gain additional income from lecturing, tutoring or supervising practicals. Part-time courses may mean that you can take on paid employment at the same time.

STUDYING OVERSEAS

Going abroad for postgraduate education can be a fantastic opportunity to study in centres of excellence, experience another culture and see the world. Allow at least eighteen months to research and make your arrangements. Your undergraduate tutors may have international contacts or your department may run exchange schemes. The university careers centre should have a section for working and studying abroad.

You may be asked for letters of introduction, a research plan, certificates of education, medical examinations and aptitude tests. You'll probably need help from a careers advisor to track down funding too.

TAKING A GAP YEAR

A well-planned gap year can bring all kinds of benefits, including:

- **An initiative test**

- **Eye-opening travel experiences**

- **A break from academia**

- **Chances to learn new languages**

- **Time to think about your future**

- **The chance to help others**

- **Experience of fund-raising**

There may be a down side to a gap year too:

- **A year on a beach doesn't impress employers**

- **Debts may get out of control**

- **Can be hard to re-adjust to life back home**

WHAT DO YOU WANNA DO?

Try any one or a combination of the following:

- **Independent travel**

- **Expeditions**

- **Voluntary work**

- **Paid work**

- **Teaching English as a foreign language (TEFL)**

Taking a Gap Year by Susan Griffith, Vacation Work, £11.95, lists the main players in the world of gap-placement organisations. Chat to other people who've already taken a gap year. Use message boards on websites like www.gapyear.com and www.yearoutgroup.org.

RIGHT, THAT'S IT, I'M OFF

Not so fast, mate. Price up transport, hotels and hostels, visas, insurance, a backpack, fees to gap organisations and living expenses.

Funding may be attached to certain programmes. Raise money by writing to local businesses or doing a sponsored stunt. Many gappers take crappy jobs in the UK to get money together before travelling or do casual work abroad.

You also need to sort out:

- **Placements for work and volunteering**
  It can take a while to find a suitable placement and complete all the necessary paperwork. Think hard about the place you want to visit, accommodation arrangements and backups if something goes wrong.

- **Tickets for travel**
  If visiting several places, you might need a round-the-world ticket. Compare different operators and find out what restrictions apply. In Europe or the USA, get discount coach cards or railcards such as an InterRail Pass. Contact specialist travel organisations such as STA Travel (www.statravel.co.uk) and Trailfinders (www.trailfinders.co.uk).

- **Visas and work permits**
  These may be tricky to obtain for some countries. If you're going to be travelling as part of an organised gap year programme, this is where a larger organisation comes in handy for expert advice.

- **Comprehensive insurance**
  Never skimp on insurance. Cover health and belongings, and if you're planning to go white-water rafting or bungee jumping then make sure it's covered in the small print.

- **Your healthcare**
  If you're going to be away for long, have check-ups with doctor and dentist before leaving. Take plenty of medication for long-standing conditions. Arrange any vaccinations well in advance.

- **Luggage and packing**
  Travel as light as you can. Take comfortable clothes in breathable materials, washbag, towel, small daypack, change of shoes, body belt to keep valuables hidden, camera and small first-aid kit. You may need water purification tablets or equipment, insect repellent, sun block and hat.

- **Your local knowledge**
  Find out about the culture you're visiting and respect local traditions. Learn enough of the language to get by, including 'please' and 'thank you'.

- **Qualifications**
  Be careful which TEFL qualification you take before leaving because some of them are recognised internationally and others aren't.

- **Accommodation**
  If you're travelling independently, book decent accommodation for the first night or two, then start searching for cheaper places.

- **Your career**
  If you've been offered a graduate position, but still want a gap year, you may be allowed to defer for one year. Speak to them as soon as you can.

Whatever you decide to do, enjoy yourself and good luck!

APPENDIX: THE BASICS

Here are the basics for your home, electricals, car and bike.

ELECTRICAL KNOW-HOW
Basic safety:

- **Never handle electrical equipment or sockets with wet hands or anything metallic.**
- **Don't overload wall sockets with too many appliances.**
- **Never do any rewiring yourself.**

If the lights go out:

- **It could be a general power cut or an electrical circuit could have tripped out.**
- **See if neighbours are affected – if not, it's a problem inside your house.**
- **Check your fuse box, usually near the electricity meter.**
- **If the trip switch is on the 'on' position, turn it off and then back on again. If power stays off, press 'test' button – if this puts trip switch into the 'off' position there's trouble with wiring or an appliance. If it doesn't go into the 'off' position, contact electricity provider.**
- **If the trip switch is in 'off' position, try switching it back on again – if it switches itself back off, this suggests a faulty electrical appliance.**
- **Turn off all electrical appliances and push trip switch back to 'on'.**
- **Switch electrical appliances back on one at a time. If trip switch goes 'off' when you get to a particular appliance, unplug and get it checked by an electrician.**

COMPUTER CARE

- Use an extension plug with circuit breaker to protect your computer from power surges.

- Use the 'defragment' and 'empty trash' functions regularly.

- Pay extra for latest versions of virus protection programs.

- If you have broadband, get a firewall.

CAR BASICS

Before a journey:

- Look under car to spot oil or water leaks.

- Top up water for windscreen washers.

- Check headlights, tail lights and brake lights.

- Check tyres for wear or damage.

- Check levels of engine oil, engine coolant and brake fluid.

- As you pull away from your parking spot, gently test brakes.

BICYCLE BASICS

On bike journeys:

- Always wear a helmet, front and rear lights and high visibility clothing.

- Carry a spare inner tube, a pump, tyre levers and spare batteries for your lights.

- Check the brakes, tyres and chain.

FIRST-AID BASICS

- Stop nosebleeds by sitting still, tilting head forwards slightly and pinching nostrils together for ten minutes. Call 999 if bleeding lasts over thirty minutes.

- **Wipe small cuts and grazes with antiseptic and gauze, then cover with sticking plaster. For cuts over 1cm deep, consult doctor.**

- **Run burns and scalds under cold water for ten minutes to get the heat out. Use lukewarm water on larger burns. Never put butter or oily lotions on a burn. If it's fairly small but bigger than a 10p piece, cover with loose dressing and see a nurse. If it covers a large part of the body, call an ambulance.**

- **Bring down swelling over bruises and sprains with an ice pack or a bag of frozen peas. There may be a broken bone underneath the swelling and medical attention will be needed.**

Deep cuts:

- **Expose the cut area. Push edges of wound together, using clean dressing if possible.**

- **Raise affected limb to help stop bleeding. Call ambulance.**

Asthma attack:

- **Be reassuring and sit the person down on a chair.**

- **Help them find and use their inhaler.**

- **If inhaler doesn't help, call an ambulance.**

Major fits (seizures):

- **If the person is unconscious or semi-conscious and lying down, get them onto a carpet or put coats or cushions underneath them so they don't hit their head on a hard surface.**

- **Loosen collars, belts or other tight clothing. Remove any sharp objects nearby.**

- **Do not restrain the person, force anything into their mouth to keep it open or pull on their tongue. These can make the situation worse.**

- If possible, roll them into the recovery position (see below).
- Call an ambulance.

Collapse:

- Check their breathing. If they're not breathing, call for help immediately. If you know cardiopulmonary resuscitation (CPR or mouth to mouth) administer it. If not, turn them onto their side and wait for help.
- If they're breathing, loosen tight clothing and put them into recovery position (on their left side and with right arm and right leg bent). See diagram below. Call ambulance and keep checking them.

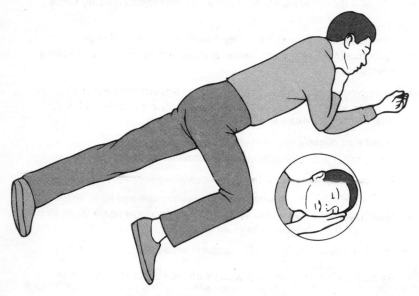

Copyright St John Ambulance 2003

LAUNDRY

Using a machine:

- Sort clothes out into two piles, light and dark colours, to wash separately. Check washing care labels on every item.

- Place one wash inside the machine; don't overfill.

- Read instructions on laundry detergent packaging.

- Close door and drawer, choose programme (only as hot as clothes can take).

- Wash new jeans separately from other clothes for first couple of washes as dye in them could stain other garments.

- Hang up laundry quickly to dry.

Hand washing:

- Fill a bowl with lukewarm water and add a small cupful of washing powder to it.

- Put clothing into the bowl and rub items against each other for a few minutes in the soapy water. Pay attention to areas that get heavy soiling, such as collars, cuffs or underarms.

- Refill bowl with cool water. Rinse the clothes thoroughly until the soapy feeling has completely gone from the water.

- Wring the clothes out and squeeze them to get as much water out of them as possible.

- Hang the clothes up to dry, remembering that they might drip.

Tumble-dryers:

- Remove anything from your wash with 'do not tumble-dry' labels.

- Wring out anything that's dripping wet.

- **Put the rest of your clothes into the tumble dryer, and switch on.**

- **Check every twenty minutes to see if contents are dry.**

Ironing:

- **Check labels, to know correct heat. If in doubt, use coolest setting.**

- **Set up ironing board and make sure base of iron is clean.**

- **Put water into iron if you want to use steam.**

- **Lay clothing flat on the ironing board and run the iron smoothly over the surface of the fabric until all the creases are gone.**

- **When ironing a complicated garment like a shirt, iron the collar and the shoulders first, then the sleeves, then the front and back of the shirt.**

- **Hang clothing up immediately to prevent new creases forming.**

STAIN REMOVAL

For general stains and spills, act quickly. Blot liquid spills up firmly from carpets and clothes using absorbent kitchen paper, until they become as dry as possible. Don't scrub, it grinds stains further into fabric or carpet pile. After blotting, use the right cleaning agent (see list below). Take care when using commercial carpet cleaners – they can change the colour of your carpet.

COMMON STAINS

Red wine: Blot firmly out of carpet or clothing using kitchen paper. Sponge carpet area with sparkling water and blot again, then use a carpet cleaner and rinse well. For clothes, rinse well in fresh water, then wash as usual.

Vomit: For carpets, wear rubber gloves and scrape up lumpy bits with blunt knife. Blot remainder with kitchen paper, then wash carpet with a mixture of warm water and detergent. Blot again. If it's smelly afterwards, use

Shake'n'Vac or Febreze. For clothes, rinse thoroughly in cold running water then wash with biological powder.

Pasta sauce: For carpets, scrape off, then rinse with bicarbonate of soda solution (1 teaspoon of powder in 500ml water), then use carpet cleaner. For clothes, rinse under cold tap until it goes pink, rub on Vanish, then wash with biological powder.

Curry: For carpets, scrape, then use carpet cleaner. Work from the outside of the stain inwards towards centre. For clothes, sponge with washing-up liquid or detergent, then rub on stain remover and wash with biological powder. Big stains may not come out.

Make-up: For carpets, scrape or vacuum up, then use carpet stain remover, followed by carpet shampoo. For clothes, try washing-up liquid or gentle detergent, then stain remover like vanish before a normal wash.

Blood: For carpets, wear rubber gloves, blot with kitchen paper, then sponge with cold water. For clothes and bedding, soak overnight in solution of cold water and washing powder. Then machine wash as normal using water as hot as fabric can take.

Ink: For carpets, blot with kitchen paper, then sponge area with cold water or bicarbonate solution and blot dry. Repeat until you've removed as much as possible, then use carpet cleaner. For clothes, rinse thoroughly under the cold tap, then treat with Vanish stain remover or Stain Devils for ink or ballpoint pen, then wash as normal in hot water.

Candle wax: For carpets, let wax solidify, then pick off as much as you can. Place a couple of sheets of kitchen paper over the area and place an iron gently over the top. Using a very low heat, melt the wax and let it absorb into the paper. Repeat process with fresh sheets of kitchen paper. For clothes, remove the wax in the same way with an iron, then wash as hot as fabric allows.

Mud: For carpets, allow to dry, then remove with stiff brush and vacuum cleaner. For clothes, brush off what you can, soak in cold water overnight, then machine wash as usual.

Grass stains: For clothes, use a Stain Devil for grass or rub on some Vanish stain remover, then add to your usual wash with some biological liquid or powder.

Coffee/tea: For carpets, blot with kitchen paper, then sponge with plenty of cold water. Use carpet shampoo for any stubborn marks. For clothes, rinse under hot tap, then machine wash in water that's as hot as the fabric allows.

GENERAL CLEANING

- **Get a kit together for spills: bowl or bucket, clean cloths, sponge, all-purpose cleaning fluid (no bleach), rubber gloves and gentle carpet cleaner.**

- **Never mix different cleaning products together – some combine to produce poisonous gases.**

Dusting:

- **You don't need fancy products to dust. Use a slightly damp, wrung-out cloth.**

Vacuuming:

- **Vacuum main areas, under furniture and around the edge of the skirting board.**

- **If your vacuum cleaner isn't picking dust up very well, check the bag or dust collector.**

Floor cleaning:

- **Laminate floors just need sweeping and wiping down with a damp cloth.**

- **Floors with vinyl or ceramic tiles need to be swept, then mopped. Use multi-purpose cleaner to make up a bucket of cleaning solution, scrub with mop. Use neat cleaner on small sticky dirty areas. Discard dirty water and rinse mop out thoroughly. Mop again using clean hot water. Leave floor to dry.**

BATHROOM STUFF

Sinks, baths and showers:

- **Use multi-purpose cleaning fluid to wipe inside and outside sinks, baths and shower trays. Pay extra attention to taps and tide marks. Pull hairs out of plugholes, rinse thoroughly with clean water.**

- **If bath is enamel, make sure cleaning products are suitable.**

- **If there's mould growing, put on rubber gloves and use mould and mildew spray.**

Toilets:

- **Wipe down seat, cistern and the outside of the bowl with multi-purpose cleaning fluid.**

- **Squirt toilet cleaner into bowl and up under the rim of toilet. Leave for a few minutes; scrub off firmly with toilet brush.**

Limescale (chalky stuff that builds up around taps, shower heads etc.):

- **Soak cloth in distilled white vinegar and wrap around affected area for a few minutes. Scrub off and rinse with clean water.**

- **Stubborn deposits need commercial cleaners like Limelite.**

CLEANING TIPS FOR KITCHENS

- **Keep kitchen cleaning equipment separate from other cleaning equipment to prevent spread of bacteria.**

- **Wipe down surfaces, outside of cookers, fridge doors and insides of microwaves with anti-bacterial cleanser.**

- **Keep sink drains free from greasy blockages by using commercial sink cleaners regularly.**

Cooker tops and hobs:

- **Take off removable metal pan holders, scrub hob with plastic scourer and multi-purpose cleaning solution. Wash pan holders in same solution. Scrape stubborn deposits gently with blunt knife.**

- **If food is badly burnt on, use commercial oven cleaner and handle with caution.**

Inside ovens:

- **Take out metal trays and racks. Scrape food out of bottom of oven with a spatula.**

- **Use a commercial oven cleaner. Be VERY careful – follow safety instructions.**

- **Scrub trays and racks with washing-up liquid, or soak in a solution of hot water and biological laundry powder.**

Pans with burnt-on food:

- **Scrape burnt food into bin, rinse pan with water and washing-up liquid.**

- **Leave pan to soak overnight filled with distilled white vinegar or hot water mixed with biological washing powder.**

Fridges:

- **Wash any stains or sticky deposits with hot water and anti-bacterial cleaning fluid.**

BINS:

- Wipe lids regularly with anti-bacterial cleanser.

- Swill out inside with solution of hot water and washing-up liquid, then wipe down with anti-bacterial cleanser.

FOOD SAFETY

- Check sell-by and use-by dates when you're buying – especially fish, poultry, meat and dairy products.

- Keep fridge temperature below 5 degrees. Don't store raw and cooked food next to each other and uncovered.

- Wash hands with soap before cooking and after handling raw meat, fish or chicken.

- Use disposable cloths to clean kitchen or cloths that are washed regularly and hung up at night to dry completely.

CONTACTS

GENERAL
National Union of Students
Nelson Mandela House
461 Holloway Road
London N7 6LJ
Tel: 020 7272 8900
Fax: 020 7263 5713
Website: www.nusonline.org.uk
email: nusuk@nus.org.uk

Citizens Advice Bureaux
Your nearest bureau will be listed in your local phone book or you can look it up online at: www.nacab.org.uk.
Advice website: www.adviceguide.org.uk

HOUSING
Shelter
88 Old Street
London EC1V 9HU

Shelter Scotland
4th Floor, Scotiabank House
6 South Charlotte Street
Edinburgh EH2 4AW

Shelter Cymru
25 Walter Road
Swansea SA15 NN

Shelterline: 0808 800 4444. Calls are free, and service includes minicom (textphone) and translators.

Main website: www.shelter.org.uk, consumer advice: www.shelternet.co.uk

MONEY
Student Loans Company
100 Bothwell Street
Glasgow G2 7JD
Tel: 0800 40 50 10
Minicom: 0800 085 3950.
Website: www.slc.co.uk

The Student Debtline
Tel: 0800 328 1813, open 8 a.m.–8 p.m., Monday to Friday

WORK AND CAREERS
Department for Education and Skills
Sanctuary Buildings
Great Smith Street
London SW1P 3BT
Public Enquiries: 0870 000 2288
Website: www.dfes.gov.uk

EQUAL OPPORTUNITIES
SKILL, the National Bureau for Students with Disabilities
Chapter House
18–20 Crucifix Lane
London SE1 3JW
Telephone or minicom: 020 7450 0620
Fax: 020 7450 0650.
Information Service, telephone: 0800 328 5050 (freephone) and 020 7657 2337, open Monday to Thursday afternoons.
Website: www.skill.org.uk

London Lesbian and Gay Switchboard
PO Box 7324
London N1 9QS
Helpline: 020 7837 7324
Admin Line: 020 7837 6768
Fax: 020 7837 7300
Website: www.llgs.org.uk
Email: admin@llgs.org.uk

Campaign for Racial Equality
St Dunstan's House
201–211 Borough High Street
London SE1 1GZ
Tel: 020 7939 0000
Fax: 020 7939 0001
Website: www.cre.gov.uk
Email: info@cre.gov.uk

HEALTH
NHS Direct
Speak to a trained nurse for advice and information about anything health-related.
Helpline: 0845 46 47 (open 24 hrs daily)
Website: www.nhsdirect.nhs.uk

Brook Advisory Service
Find out about what your contraception options are and what services are available in your local area.
Tel: 0800 0185 023 (open 9 a.m.–5 p.m. Monday to Friday)
Website: www.brook.org.uk

CRIME AND SAFETY
Victim Support
Victim Supportline: 0845 30 30 900, open 9 a.m–9 p.m. Monday to Friday, 9 a.m.–7 p.m. weekends and 9 a.m.–5 p.m. bank holidays

Minicom: 020 7896 3776
Website: www.victimsupport.com

The Suzy Lamplugh Trust
National Centre for Personal Safety
Hampton House
20 Albert Embankment
London SE1 7TJ
Tel: 020 7091 0014
Website: www.suzylamplugh.org.

THANKS

Many thanks to all at Virgin Books Ltd, and to everyone who proofread the first and second editions of this book. I also gratefully acknowledge the Suzy Lamplugh Trust and Shelter who provided so much information for the Safety and Housing chapters. Special second edition gratitude goes to Alka Mehta and Kate Spector for providing flat foods, general encouragement and a sprinkle of fabulousness, and to Messrs Jose Cuervo and Charles Tanqueray for the after party.